# STATISM

## *The Shadows of Another Night*

EDITED BY
CHARLIE RODRIGUEZ

FORTRESS
BOOK | SERVICE

Tanglewood Publishing

STATISM: THE SHADOWS OF ANOTHER NIGHT

edited by
Charlie Rodriguez

Copyright © 2015 by Tanglewood Publishing

ISBN-13: 978-0-9852897-8-2

Tanglewood Publishing
800-241-4016

Cover Layout and Design by Christy Rodriguez
Book Design and Layout by Mieke Moller

Printed in the United States of America

# CONTENTS

# EDITOR'S NOTE

Two works gave me a clear understanding of the purpose of this anthology. First was R.C. Sproul's classic article "Statism" with this definition:

> A decline from statehood to statism happens when the government is perceived as or claims to be the ultimate reality. This reality then replaces God as the supreme entity upon which human existence depends.

Second was President Eisenhower's warning of "the shadows of another night" from his First Inaugural Address.

Eisenhower understood that victory in Europe, victory over evil Nazism, would come at a high cost. He also understood that given the right set of circumstances, the horrors he had personally witnessed could happen again. How to prevent this recurrence, I think, was one of his greatest concerns.

This should be our greatest concern, too, when governments and leaders move toward totalitarian control, and when citizens, especially religious leaders, do not respond openly and with moral principle and outrage — whether due to fear, naiveté, passivity, or a combination of all three.

Nevertheless—and it is the bold assertion of this anthology and of the editor-there is nothing in the history of mankind that warrants this type of thinking and inaction on the part of citizens and religious leaders when face-to-face with evil. The most important thing to remember is that reaction against statism is, and always has been, firmly established in God's Word.

*Charlie Rodriguez, Editor*

# STATISM
## The Biggest Concern for the Future of the Church in America

BY R.C. SPOUL

"A DECREE WENT OUT FROM CAESAR AUGUSTUS that all the world should be registered...." In Luke 2, the well-known passage introducing the nativity story, the title accorded to the Roman emperor is Caesar Augustus. Had this census been mandated earlier under the monarchy of Julius Caesar, the Scripture would read: "A decree went out from Julius Caesar...." Had Octavian followed the model of Julius, he would have called himself Octavianus Caesar, and then the text would read: "A decree went out from Octavianus Caesar...." But we note Octavius' explicit change of his personal name to the title Caesar Augustus. This indicates the emerging dimension of the emperor cult in Rome, by which those who were elevated to the role of emperor were worshiped as deities. To be called "august" would mean to be clothed with supreme dignity, to which is owed the reverence given to the sacred. The elevation of the emperor in Rome to this kind of status was the ancient zenith of statism.

About thirty years ago, I shared a taxi cab in St. Louis with Francis Schaeffer. I had known Dr. Schaeffer for many years, and he had been instrumental in helping us begin our ministry in Ligonier, Pennsylvania, in 1971. Since our time together in St. Louis was during the twilight of Schaeffer's career,

I posed this question to him: "Dr. Schaeffer, what is your biggest concern for the future of the church in America?" Without hesitation, Dr. Schaeffer turned to me and spoke one word: "Statism." Schaeffer's biggest concern at that point in his life was that the citizens of the United States were beginning to invest their country with supreme authority, such that the free nation of America would become one that would be dominated by a philosophy of the supremacy of the state.

In statism, we see the suffix "ism," which indicates a philosophy or world-view. A decline from statehood to statism happens when the government is perceived as or claims to be the ultimate reality. This reality then replaces God as the supreme entity upon which human existence depends.

In the nineteenth century, Hegel argued in his extensive and complex study of Western history that progress represents the unfolding in time and space of the absolute Idea (Hegel's vague understanding of God), which would reach its apex in the creation of the Prussian state. The assumption that Hegel made in the nineteenth century was made before the advent of Hitler's Third Reich, Stalin's Russia, and Chairman Mao's communist China. These nations reached an elevation of statism never dreamed of by Hegel in his concept of the Prussian state.

In America, we have a long history of valuing the concept of the separation of church and state. This idea historically referred to a division of labors between the church and the civil magistrate. However, initially both the church and the state were seen as entities ordained by God and subject to His governance. In that sense, the state was considered to be an entity that was "under God." What has happened in the past few decades is the obfuscation of this original distinction between church and state, so that today the language we hear of separation of church and state, when carefully exegeted, communicates the idea of the separation of the state from God. In this sense, it's not merely that the state declares independence from the church, it also declares independence from God and presumes itself to rule with autonomy.

The whole idea of a nation under God has been challenged again and again, and we have seen the exponential growth of government in our land, particularly the federal government, so that the government now virtually engulfs all of life. Where education once was under the direction of local authorities, it now is controlled and directed by federal legislation. The economy that once was driven by the natural forces of the market has now come under the strict control of the federal government, which not only regulates the economy, but considers itself responsible for controlling it. Where we have seen the largest measure of the loss of liberty is with respect to the function of the church. Though the church is still somewhat tolerated in America (in a way it was not tolerated in Mao's Red China and under Stalin), it is tolerated only when it remains outside of the public square. In other words, the church has been relegated to a status not unlike that given to the native Americans, where the tribes were allowed to continue to exist as long as they functioned safely on a reservation, outside of any significant influence on the government. So although the church has not been banished completely by the statism that has emerged in America, it has been effectively banished from the public square.

Throughout the history of the Christian church, Christianity has always stood over against all forms of statism. Statism is the natural and ultimate enemy to Christianity because it involves a usurpation of the reign of God. If Francis Schaeffer was right - and each year that passes makes his prognosis seem all the more accurate - it means that the church and the nation face a serious crisis in our day. In the final analysis, if statism prevails in America, it will mean not only the death of our religious freedom, but also the death of the state itself. We face perilous times where Christians and all people need to be vigilant about the rapidly encroaching elevation of the state to supremacy.

--------------------------

*Robert Charles Sproul is an American Reformed theologian, author, and pastor. He is the founder and chairman and can be heard daily on the Renewing Your Mind radio broadcast in the United States and internationally.*

[Permission to reprint granted to Fortress Book Service by Ligonier Ministries]

# INAUGURAL ADDRESS
## January 20, 1953

### DWIGHT DAVID EISENHOWER

34th President of the United States
Commander Allied Forces,
D-Day, June 6, 1944, Normandy Invasion

[Delivered in person at the Capitol]

MY FRIENDS, BEFORE I BEGIN the expression of those thoughts that I deem appropriate to this moment, would you permit me the privilege of uttering a little private prayer of my own. And I ask that you bow your heads:

Almighty God, as we stand here at this moment my future associates in the Executive branch of Government join me in beseeching that Thou will make full and complete our dedication to the service of the people in this throng, and their fellow citizens everywhere.

Give us, we pray, the power to discern clearly right from wrong, and allow all our words and actions to be governed thereby, and by the laws of this land. Especially we pray that our concern shall be for all the people regardless of station, race or calling.

May cooperation be permitted and be the mutual aim of those who, under the concepts of our Constitution, hold to differing political faiths; so that all may work for the good of our beloved country and Thy glory. Amen.

My fellow citizens:

The world and we have passed the midway point of a century of continuing challenge. We sense with all our faculties that forces of good and evil are massed and armed and opposed as rarely before in history.

This fact defines the meaning of this day. We are summoned by this honored and historic ceremony to witness more than the act of one citizen swearing his oath of service, in the presence of God. We are called as a people to give testimony in the sight of the world to our faith that the future shall belong to the free.

Since this century's beginning, a time of tempest has seemed to come upon the continents of the earth. Masses of Asia have awakened to strike off shackles of the past. Great nations of Europe have fought their bloodiest wars. Thrones have toppled and their vast empires have disappeared. New nations have been born.

For our own country, it has been a time of recurring trial. We have grown in power and in responsibility. We have passed through the anxieties of depression and of war to a summit unmatched in man's history. Seeking to secure peace in the world, we have had to fight through the forests of the Argonne to the shores of Iwo Jima, and to the cold mountains of Korea.

In the swift rush of great events, we find ourselves groping to know the full sense and meaning of these times in which we live. In our quest of understanding, we beseech God's guidance. We summon all our knowledge of the past and we scan all signs of the future. We bring all our wit and all our will to meet the question:

How far have we come in man's long pilgrimage from darkness toward the light? Are we nearing the light—a day of freedom and of peace for all mankind? Or are the shadows of another night closing in upon us?

Great as are the preoccupations absorbing us at home, concerned as we are with matters that deeply affect our livelihood today and our vision of the future, each of these domestic problems is dwarfed by, and often even created by, this question that involves all humankind.

This trial comes at a moment when man's power to achieve good or to inflict evil surpasses the brightest hopes and the sharpest fears of all ages. We can turn rivers in their courses, level mountains to the plains. Oceans and land and sky are avenues for our colossal commerce. Disease diminishes and life lengthens.

Yet the promise of this life is imperiled by the very genius that has made it possible. Nations amass wealth. Labor sweats to create—and turns out devices to level not only mountains but also cities. Science seems ready to confer upon us, as its final gift, the power to erase human life from this planet.

At such a time in history, we who are free must proclaim anew our faith. This faith is the abiding creed of our fathers. It is our faith in the deathless dignity of man, governed by eternal moral and natural laws.

This faith defines our full view of life. It establishes, beyond debate, those gifts of the Creator that are man's inalienable rights, and that make all men equal in His sight.

In the light of this equality, we know that the virtues most cherished by free people—love of truth, pride of work, devotion to country—all are treasures equally precious in the lives of the most humble and of the most exalted. The men who mine coal and fire furnaces, and balance ledgers, and turn lathes, and pick cotton, and heal the sick and plant corn—all serve as proudly and as profitably for America as the statesmen who draft treaties and the legislators who enact laws.

This faith rules our whole way of life. It decrees that we, the people, elect leaders not to rule but to serve. It asserts that we have the right to choice of our own work and to the reward of our own toil. It inspires the initiative that makes our productivity the wonder of the world. And it warns that any man who seeks to deny equality among all his brothers betrays the spirit of the free and invites the mockery of the tyrant.

It is because we, all of us, hold to these principles that the political changes accomplished this day do not imply turbulence, upheaval or disorder. Rather this change expresses a purpose of strengthening our dedication and devotion to the precepts of our founding documents, a conscious renewal of faith in our country and in the watchfulness of a Divine Providence.

The enemies of this faith know no god but force, no devotion but its use. They tutor men in treason. They feed upon the hunger of others. Whatever defies them, they torture, especially the truth.

Here, then, is joined no argument between slightly differing philosophies. This conflict strikes directly at the faith of our fathers and the lives of our sons. No principle or treasure that we hold, from the spiritual knowledge of our free schools and churches to the creative magic of free labor and capital, nothing lies safely beyond the reach of this struggle.

**Freedom is pitted against slavery; lightness against the dark**

The faith we hold belongs not to us alone but to the free of all the world. This common bond binds the grower of rice in Burma and the planter of wheat in Iowa, the shepherd in southern Italy and the mountaineer in the Andes. It confers a common dignity upon the French soldier who dies in Indo-China, the British soldier killed in Malaya, the American life given in Korea.

We know, beyond this, that we are linked to all free peoples not merely by a noble idea but by a simple need. No free people can for long cling to any privilege or enjoy any safety in economic solitude. For all our own material might, even we need markets in the world for the surpluses of our farms and our factories. Equally, we need for these same farms and factories vital materials and products of distant lands. This basic law of interdependence, so manifest in the commerce of peace, applies with thousand-fold intensity in the event of war.

So we are persuaded by necessity and by belief that the strength of all free peoples lies in unity; their danger, in discord.

To produce this unity, to meet the challenge of our time, destiny has laid upon our country the responsibility of the free world's leadership.

So it is proper that we assure our friends once again that, in the discharge of this responsibility, we Americans know and we observe the difference between world leadership and imperialism; between firmness and truculence; between a thoughtfully calculated goal and spasmodic reaction to the stimulus of emergencies.

We wish our friends the world over to know this above all: we face the threat—not with dread and confusion—but with confidence and conviction.

We feel this moral strength because we know that we are not helpless prisoners of history. We are free men. We shall remain free, never to be proven guilty of the one capital offense against freedom, a lack of stanch faith.

In pleading our just cause before the bar of history and in pressing our labor for world peace, we shall be guided by certain fixed principles. These principles are:

1.  Abhorring war as a chosen way to balk the purposes of those who threaten us, we hold it to be the first task of statesmanship to develop the strength that will deter the forces of aggression and promote the conditions of peace. For, as it must be the supreme purpose of all free men, so it must be the dedication of their leaders, to save humanity from preying upon itself. In the light of this principle, we stand ready to engage with any and all others in joint effort to remove the causes of mutual fear and distrust among nations, so as to make possible drastic reduction of armaments. The sole requisites for undertaking such effort are that—in their purpose—they be aimed logically and honestly toward secure peace for all; and that—in their result—they provide methods by which every participating nation will prove good faith in carrying out its pledge.
2.  Realizing that common sense and common decency alike dictate the futility of appeasement, we shall never try to placate an aggressor by the false and wicked bargain of trading honor for security.

Americans, indeed, all free men, remember that in the final choice a soldier's pack is not so heavy a burden as a prisoner's chains.

3. Knowing that only a United States that is strong and immensely productive can help defend freedom in our world, we view our Nation's strength and security as a trust upon which rests the hope of free men everywhere. It is the firm duty of each of our free citizens and of every free citizen everywhere to place the cause of his country before the comfort, the convenience of himself.

4. Honoring the identity and the special heritage of each nation in the world, we shall never use our strength to try to impress upon another people our own cherished political and economic institutions.

5. Assessing realistically the needs and capacities of proven friends of freedom, we shall strive to help them to achieve their own security and well-being. Likewise, we shall count upon them to assume, within the limits of their resources, their full and just burdens in the common defense of freedom.

6. Recognizing economic health as an indispensable basis of military strength and the free world's peace, we shall strive to foster everywhere, and to practice ourselves, policies that courage productivity and profitable trade. For the impoverishment of any single people in the world means danger to the well-being of all other peoples.

7. Appreciating that economic need, military security and political wisdom combine to suggest regional groupings of free peoples, we hope, within the framework of the United Nations, to help strengthen such special bonds the world over. The nature of these ties must vary with the different problems of different areas. In the Western Hemisphere, we enthusiastically join with all our neighbors in the work of perfecting a community of fraternal trust and common purpose. In Europe, we ask that enlightened and inspired leaders of the Western nations strive with renewed vigor to make the unity of their peoples a reality. Only as free Europe unitedly marshals its strength can it effectively safeguard, even with our help, its spiritual and cultural heritage.

8. Conceiving the defense of freedom, like freedom itself, to be one and indivisible, we hold all continents and peoples in equal regard and honor. We reject any insinuation that one race or another, one people or another, is in any sense inferior or expendable.

9. Respecting the United Nations as the living sign of all people's hope for peace, we shall strive to make it not merely an eloquent symbol but an effective force. And in our quest for an honorable peace, we shall neither compromise, nor tire, nor ever cease.

By these rules of conduct, we hope to be known to all peoples.

By their observance, an earth of peace may become not a vision but a fact.

This hope — this supreme aspiration — must rule the way we live.

We must be ready to dare all for our country. For history does not long entrust the care of freedom to the weak or the timid. We must acquire proficiency in defense and display stamina in purpose.

We must be willing, individually and as a Nation, to accept whatever sacrifices may be required of us. A people that values its privileges above its principles soon loses both.

These basic precepts are not lofty abstractions, far removed from matters of daily living. They are laws of spiritual strength that generate and define our material strength. Patriotism means equipped forces and a prepared citizenry. Moral stamina means more energy and more productivity, on the farm and in the factory. Love of liberty means the guarding of every resource that makes freedom possible — from the sanctity of our families and the wealth of our soil to the genius of our scientists.

And so each citizen plays an indispensable role. The productivity of our heads, our hands and our hearts is the source of all the strength we can command, for both the enrichment of our lives and the winning of the peace.

No person, no home, no community can be beyond the reach of this call. We are summoned to act in wisdom and in conscience, to work with industry, to teach with persuasion, to preach with conviction, to weigh our every deed with care and with compassion. For this truth must be clear before us: whatever America hopes to bring to pass in the world must first come to pass in the heart of America.

The peace we seek, then, is nothing less than the practice and fulfillment of our whole faith among ourselves and in our dealings with others. This signifies more than the stilling of guns, casing the sorrow of war. More than escape from death, it is a way of life. More than a haven for the weary, it is a hope for the brave.

This is the hope that beckons us onward in this century of trial. This is the work that awaits us all, to be done with bravery, with charity, and with prayer to Almighty God.

My citizens—I thank you.

-------------------------

*Note: This text follows the White House release of the address. The President spoke from a platform erected on the steps of the central east front of the Capitol. Immediately before the address the oath of office was administered by Chief Justice Fred M. Vinson.*

[Permission to reprint granted to Fortress Books Service from the Eisenhower Presidential Library.]

# THE LIMITS OF CIVIL OBEDIENCE

## From *A Christian Manifesto (1981)*

**BY FRANCIS A. SCHAEFFER**

(Crossway Books, Wheaton, IL, pp. 89-102)

THE FOUNDING FATHERS AND THOSE IN THE THIRTEEN STATES understood what they were building upon. We have reached a place today which is violently opposed to what the Founding Fathers of this country and those in the thirteen individual states had in mind when they came together and formed the union.

It is time to think to the *bottom line* as our forefathers did. What was the *bottom line* that our forefathers thought to that made it possible for them to act as they did?

First, what is the final relationship to the state on the part of anyone whose base is the existence of God? How would you answer that question?

You must understand that those in our present material-energy, chance oriented generation have no reason to obey the state except that the state has the guns and has the patronage. That is the only reason they have for obeying the state. A material-energy, chance orientation gives no base, no reason, except force and patronage, as to why citizens should obey the state.

The Christian, the God-fearing person, is not like that. The Bible tells us that God has commanded us to obey the state.

But now a second question follows very quickly. Has God set up an authority in the state that is autonomous from Himself? Are we to obey the state no matter what? Are we? In this one area is indeed Man the measure of all things? And I would answer, not at all, not at all.

When Jesus says in Matthew 22:21: "Give to Caesar what is Caesar's, and to God what is God's," it is not:

GOD and CAESAR

It was, is, and it always will be:

GOD

and

CAESAR

The civil government, as all of life, stands under the Law of God. In this fallen world God has given us certain offices to protect us from the chaos which is the natural result of that fallenness. But when any office commands that which is contrary to the Word of God, those who hold that office abrogate their authority and they are not to be obeyed. And that includes the state.

Romans 13:1-4 says:

> Do you want to be free from fear of the one in authority? Then do what is right and he will commend you. For he is God's servant to do you good. But if you do wrong, be afraid, for he does not bear the sword for nothing. He is God's servant, an agent of wrath to bring punishment on the wrongdoer.

God has ordained the state as a delegated authority; it is not autonomous. The state is to be an agent of justice, to restrain evil by punishing the wrongdoer, and to protect the good in society. When it does the reverse, it has no proper authority. It is then a usurped authority and as such it becomes lawless and is tyranny.

In 1 Peter 2:13-17 we read:

> Submit yourselves for the Lord's sake to every authority instituted
> among men: whether to the king, as the supreme authority, or to
> governors, who are sent by him to punish those who do wrong and
> to commend those who do right. For it is God's will that by doing
> good you should silence the ignorant talk of foolish men. Live as
> free men, but do not use your freedom as a cover-up for evil; live as
> servants of God. Show proper respect to everyone: Love the broth-
> erhood of believers, fear God, honor the king.

Peter says here that civil authority is to be honored and that God is to be
feared. The state, as he defines it, is to punish those who do wrong and
commend those who do right. If this is not so, then the whole structure falls
apart. Clearly, the state is to be a ministry of justice. This is the legitimate
function of the state, and in this structure Christians are to obey the state as a
matter of "conscience" (Romans 13:5).

But what is to be done when the state does that which violates its legitimate
function? The early Christians died because they would not obey the state in
a civil matter. People often say to us that the early church did not show any
civil disobedience. They do not know church history. Why were the Christians in the Roman Empire thrown to the lions? From the Christian's viewpoint it was for a religious reason. But from the viewpoint of the Roman
State they were in civil disobedience, they were civil rebels. The Roman
State did not care what anybody believed religiously; you could believe
anything, or you could be an atheist. But you had to worship Caesar as a
sign of your loyalty to the state. The Christians said they would not worship Caesar, anybody, or anything, but the living God. Thus to the Roman
Empire they were rebels, and it was civil disobedience. That is why they
were thrown to the lions.

Francis Legge in volume one of his book *Forerunners and Rivals of Christianity
from 330 B.C. to A.D. 330* writes: "The officials of the Roman Empire in times
of persecution sought to force the Christians to sacrifice, not to any heathen
gods, but to the Genius of the Emperor and the Fortune of the City of Rome;

and at all times the Christians' refusal was looked upon not as a religious but as a political offense."[1]

The *bottom line* is that at a certain point there is not only the right, but the duty, to disobey the state.

Through the ages Christians have taken the same position as did the early church in disobeying the state when it commanded what was contrary to God's Law. William Tyndale (c. 1490-1536), the English translator of the Bible, advocated the supreme authority of the Scripture over and against the state and the church. Government authorities continually sought to capture him, but Tyndale was successful in evading them for years. Tyndale was eventually condemned as a heretic, tried and executed on October 6, 1536. John Bunyan (1628-1688) was found guilty of breaking the king's law. Arrested three times for preaching without a state license and for failing to attend the Church of England, he spent twelve years in an English jail. He wrote many works from this jail cell, including *Pilgrim's Progress*.

In almost every place where the Reformation had success there was some form of civil disobedience or armed rebellion:

*Netherlands:* Catholic Spain had isolated the non-Catholic population both politically and geographically. Thus the Protestants concentrated in what is now Holland which became the last holdout against the Spanish power. The leaders of the revolt established Protestantism as the dominant religious form of the country. The turning point was the battle for Leyden in 1574. The Dutch Protestants fought a very hard and costly battle. When they finally won, the door was open not only for the subsequent political entity of Holland, but also for the successful Dutch Reformation with all its cultural as well as religious results.

*Sweden:* In 1527 the Vasa family broke away from Denmark as an act of rebellion and established Sweden as a Lutheran country. Later, in 1630, it was the Swedish king, Gustavus Adolphus, a sincere champion of Lutheranism, who marched his army out of Sweden and into Germany against the Emperor to protect Protestant Germany with his force of arms.

*Denmark:* In 1536 the Protestant party of nobles overthrew the Danish dynasty—an act of "civil disobedience" with accompanying strife. They then set up a new government and a new dynasty and established Lutheranism in the country.

*Germany:* Luther was protected by the Duke of Saxony against the political and military power of the Emperor. After many wars in which the Duke of Saxony and other German nobles kept the Emperor at bay, the Peace of Augsburg was signed in 1555. In this it was established that the ruler's religion would determine the religion of his geographical location. Thus the German Reformation won its right to exist. Later, with the rise of the Roman Catholic Counter-Reformation, the Thirty Years War was fought, and out of this came the Peace of Westphalia in 1648 which ratified the 1555 Peace of Augsburg. By this, German Protestantism was protected from the reprisals of the Counter-Reformation.

*Switzerland:* Bern established reform and Protestantism between 1523 and 1525 by Communal vote. Yet for what is now the Canton of Vaud (where I live), it was Protestant Bern's military control of this area at that time which gave William Farel his opportunity to preach the gospel in Aigle and Ollon, leading to reformation in French-speaking Switzerland.

*Geneva:* This area became Protestant by vote of the Common Council in 1533-1534. Calvin came to Geneva in 1536. There was no open war, but the Reformation was established despite the constant threat of war by the House of Savoy.

Because John Knox of Scotland is such a clear example I will give more detail concerning him.[2] Knox was ordained to the priesthood in 1536 (the year William Tyndale was executed) after studying at St. Andrews University near Edinburgh where Samuel Rutherford later was Rector. Knox was also a lawyer and a bodyguard to the fiery evangelist George Wishart.

Shortly thereafter, Knox accepted a call to the ministry and began attacking the Roman Catholic Church. This was extremely dangerous since the Roman Catholic Church exerted a dominant influence over the Scottish State. Knox was prevented from preaching on Sundays (the dates were conveniently filled by priests). Knox held services on weekdays during which he refuted what was said by others on Sundays. So successful were his efforts that a majority of those in Edinburgh made an open profession of the Protestant faith by participating in the Lord's Supper as administered by Knox.

On June 30, 1547, Knox, along with others, was captured by French forces in the war with England. Disaster that this was, it was better than what would have happened if the Scottish government had apprehended him. Most likely, he would have been burned at the stake.

After almost two years as a galley slave, Knox gained his liberty. He landed as a refugee in England in 1549 and resumed preaching. He was so effective that Protestant families in Scotland, hearing of his ministry, crossed the border illegally and resettled in Berwick, England, so as to be near him.

Knox is rightly thought of as a radical reformer. There is, however, an important distinction to keep in mind concerning him. Throughout his ministry, Knox appealed for moderation and compromise whenever truly fundamental issues were not at stake.

Attempts to keep the English crown in Protestant hands failed and in August of 1553 the Roman Catholic Mary Tudor entered London. Many of the outspoken Protestants were taken captive and imprisoned. Knox was able to escape from the country to Geneva, Switzerland.

It was during this time that Knox developed a theology of resistance to tyranny. He began smuggling pamphlets into England. The most significant of these was the *Admonition to England* (for complete title see *References* in the back of this book), published in July of 1554. With this move, he had stepped into new territory, going further than any Reformer had previously gone. Within a few years, tens of thousands of Huguenots were offering armed resistance to the French government; and the year Knox died saw the beginning of the successful revolt and saving of Holland. Knox had shocked the world with his *Admonition to England*, but he had also been convincing. Jasper Ridley in *John Knox* writes, "The theory of the justification of revolution is Knox's special contribution to theological and political thought."[3]

Whereas Reformers such as Martin Luther and John Calvin had reserved the right to rebellion to the civil rulers alone, Knox went further. He maintained that the common people had the right and duty to disobedience and rebellion if state officials ruled contrary to the Bible. To do otherwise would be rebellion against God.

Knox was not against civil government *per se*. He knew well that civil government is ordained of God. Knox maintained, however, that state officials have the duty of obeying God's Laws. He wrote: "Kings then have not an absolute power in their regiment to do what pleases them; but their power is limited by God's word."[4] A ruler must consider that he is "Lieutenant to One whose eyes watch upon him."[5] All life and all actions, he reiterated, must have their base in God's Word.

Knox finally arrived back in Scotland on May 2, 1559. Scotland became a Protestant country. The effectiveness of the Presbyterian system there was so great that the persecutions of the following century were unable to root it out. The Reformation had come to stay. And it was John Knox, an exponent of godly resistance in the face of tyranny, who planted the seeds that were later nurtured by such men as Samuel Rutherford.

In contrast to the countries named above where there was success for the Reformation—in each case involving various forms of civil disobedience or armed rebellion—one can think of where the Reformation was exterminated by force because of the lack of such protection:

*Hungary:* The Reformation had great initial success. But when the Turks pulled out of the country, the Roman Catholic authorities had unchecked power and used it to eliminate the Reformation—largely by killing off just about all of the Protestants.

*France:* The Huguenots were most successful in numbers and position. But on St. Bartholomew's Day (1572), lacking protection, the Reformation was broken in France by the mass assassination of most of its leadership.

*Spain:* There was a small Reformation movement among the monks of Seville. Lacking any protection, they were totally eliminated by martyrdom.

Thus, in almost every place where the Reformation flourished there was not only religious noncompliance, there was civil disobedience as well.

It was in this setting that Samuel Rutherford (1600-1661) wrote his *Lex, Rex, or the Law and the Prince* (1664). What is the concept in *Lex Rex*? Very simply: The law is king, and if the king and the government disobey the law they are to be disobeyed. And the law is founded on the Law of God. *Lex Rex* was outlawed in both England and Scotland. The parliament of Scotland was meeting in order to condemn Samuel Rutherford to death for his views, and the only reason he was not executed as a civil rebel is because he died first.

In his classic work, *Lex Rex*, Rutherford set forth the proper Christian response to nonbiblical acts by the state. Rutherford, a Presbyterian, was one of the Scottish commissioners at the Westminster Assembly in London (1643-1647) and later became Rector at St. Andrews University in Scotland. The book *Lex Rex*, in a society of landed classes and monarchy, created an immediate controversy.

The governing authorities were concerned about *Lex Rex* because of its attack on the undergirding foundation of seventeenth century political government in Europe—"the divine right of kings." This doctrine held that the king or state ruled as God's appointed regent and, this being so, the king's word was law. Placed against this position was Rutherford's assertion that the basic premise of civil government and, therefore, law, must be based on God's Law as given in the Bible. As such, Rutherford argued, all men, even the king, are *under* the Law and not above it. This concept was considered political rebellion and punishable as treason.

Rutherford argued that Romans 13 indicates that all power is from God and that government is ordained and instituted by God. The state, however, is to be administered according to the principles of God's Law. Acts of the state which contradicted God's Law were illegitimate and acts of tyranny. Tyranny was defined as ruling without the sanction of God.

Rutherford held that a tyrannical government is always immoral. He said that "a power ethical, politic, or moral, to oppress, is not from God, and is not a power, but a licentious deviation of a power; and is no more from God, but from sinful nature and the old serpent, than a license to sin."[6]

Rutherford presents several arguments to establish the right and duty of resistance to unlawful government.[7] *First,* since tyranny is satanic, not to resist it is to resist God—to resist tyranny is to honor God. *Second,* since the ruler is granted power conditionally, it follows that the people have the power to withdraw their sanction if the proper conditions are not fulfilled. The civil magistrate is a "fiduciary figure"—that is, he holds his authority in trust for the people. Violation of the trust gives the people a legitimate base for resistance.

It follows from Rutherford's thesis that citizens have the *moral* obligation to resist unjust and tyrannical government. While we must always be subject to the *office* of the magistrate, we are not to be subject to the *man* in that office who commands that which is contrary to the Bible.

Rutherford offered suggestions concerning illegitimate acts of the state. A ruler, he wrote, should not be deposed merely because he commits a single breach of the compact he has with the people. Only when the magistrate acts in such a way that the governing structure of the country is being destroyed—that is, when he is attacking the fundamental structure of society—is he to be relieved of his power and authority.

That is exactly what we are facing today. The whole structure of our society is being attacked and destroyed. It is being given an entirely opposite base which gives exactly opposite results. The reversal is much more total and destructive than that which Rutherford or any of the Reformers faced in their day.

---------------------------

*Francis August Schaeffer was an American Evangelical Christian theologian, philosopher, and Presbyterian pastor. He is most famous for his writings and his establishment of the L'Abri community in Switzerland.*

[1]Francis Legge, *Forerunners and Rivals of Christianity from 330 B.C. to 330 A.C.*, vol. 1 (New Hyde Park, NY: University Books, 1964), p. xxiv.

[2]The following section on John Knox, pp. 95-101, draws upon material which first appeared in an essay by David H. Chilton in "John Knox," *Journal of Christian Reconstruction*, vol. 5 (Winter 1978-79), pp. 194-206; reprinted here with the permission of the author.

[3]Jasper Ridley, *John Knox* (New York: Oxford, 1968), p. 171

[4, 5]John Knox, *Works* (New York: AMS Press, Vol. vi, 1968), pp.236-238.

[6]Samuel Rutherford, *Lex Rex, or, The Law and the Prince* (n.p., 1644), published in vol. 3 *The Presbyterian Armoury* (1846), p. 34.

[7]The following section on Samuel Rutherford, pp. 101-104, draws upon material which appeared in an essay by Richard Flin in "Samuel Rutherford and Puritan Political Theory," *Journal of Christian Reconstruction*, vol. 5 (Winter 1978-79), pp. 49-74.

# IS PROGRESS POSSIBLE?
## Willing Slaves of the Welfare State

**BY C.S. LEWIS**

from God in the Dock (Eerdmans, 1983)

PROGRESS MEANS MOVEMENT IN A DESIRED DIRECTION, and we do not all desire the same things for our species. In 'Possible Worlds" Professor Haldane [1- One essay in J. B. S. Haldane's Possible Worlds and Other Essays (London, 1927). See also 'The Last Judgment' in the same book.] pictured a future in which Man, foreseeing that Earth would soon be uninhabitable, adapted himself for migration to Venus by drastically modifying his physiology and abandoning justice, pity and happiness. The desire here is for mere survival. Now I care far more how humanity lives than how long. Progress, for me, means increasing goodness and happiness of individual lives. For the species, as for each man, mere longevity seems to me a contemptible ideal.

I therefore go even further than C. P. Snow in removing the H-bomb from the centre of the picture. Like him, I am not certain whether if it killed one-third of us (the one-third I belong to), this would be a bad thing for the remainder; like him, I don't think it will kill us all. But suppose it did? As a Christian I take it for granted that human history will some day end; and I am offering Omniscience no advice as to the best date for that consummation. I am more concerned by what the Bomb is doing already.

One meets young people who make the threat of it a reason for poisoning every pleasure and evading every duty in the present. Didn't they know that, Bomb or no Bomb, all men die (many in horrible ways)? There's no good moping and sulking about it.

Having removed what I think a red herring, I return to the real question. Are people becoming, or likely to become, better or happier? Obviously this allows only the most conjectural answer. Most individual experience (and there is no other kind) never gets into the news, let alone the history books; one has an imperfect grasp even of one's own. We are reduced to generalities. Even among these it is hard to strike a balance. Sir Charles enumerates many real ameliorations. Against these we must set Hiroshima, Black and Tans, Gestapo, Ogpu, brain-washing, the Russian slave camps. Perhaps we grow kinder to children; but then we grow less kind to the old. Any G.P.[2-A general practitioner (doctor)] will tell you that even prosperous people refuse to look after their parents. 'Can't they be got into some sort of Home?' says Goneril. [3- In Shakespeare's King Lear]

More useful, I think, than an attempt at balancing, is the reminder that most of these phenomena, good and bad, are made possible by two things. These two will probably determine most of what happens to us for some time.

The first is the advance, and increasing application, of science. As a means to the ends I care for, this is neutral. We shall grow able to cure, and to produce, more diseases—bacterial war, not bombs, might ring down the curtain—to alleviate, and to inflict, more pains, to husband, or to waste, the resources of the planet more extensively. We can become either more beneficent or more mischievous. My guess is we shall do both; mending one thing and marring another, removing old miseries and producing new ones, safeguarding ourselves here and endangering ourselves there.

The second is the changed relation between Government and subjects. Sir Charles mentions our new attitude to crime. I will mention the trainloads of Jews delivered at the German gas-chambers. It seems shocking to suggest a common element, but I think one exists. On the humanitarian view all crime is pathological; it demands not retributive punishment but cure. This separates the criminal's treatment from the concepts of justice and desert; a 'just cure' is meaningless.

On the old view public opinion might protest against a punishment (it protested against our old penal code) as excessive, more than the man 'deserved'; an ethical question on which anyone might have an opinion. But a remedial treatment can be judged only by the probability of its success; a technical question on which only experts can speak.

Thus the criminal ceases to be a person, a subject of rights and duties, and becomes merely an object on which society can work. And this is, in principle, how Hitler treated the Jews. They were objects; killed not for ill desert but because, on his theories, they were a disease in society. If society can mend, remake, and unmake men at its pleasure, its pleasure may, of course, be humane or homicidal. The difference is important. But, either way, rulers have become owners. Observe how the 'humane' attitude to crime could operate. If crimes are diseases, why should diseases be treated differently from crimes? And who but the experts can define disease? One school of psychology regards my religion as a neurosis. If this neurosis ever becomes inconvenient to Government, what is to prevent my being subjected to a compulsory 'cure'? It may be painful; treatments sometimes are. But it will be no use asking, 'What have I done to deserve this?' The Straightener will reply: 'But, my dear fellow, no one's blaming you. We no longer believe in retributive justice. We're healing you.'

This would be no more than an extreme application of the political philosophy implicit in most modern communities. It has stolen on us unawares. Two wars necessitated vast curtailments of liberty, and we have grown, though grumblingly, accustomed to our chains. The increasing complexity and precariousness of our economic life have forced Government to take over many spheres of activity once left to choice or chance. Our intellectuals have surrendered first to the slave-philosophy of Hegel, then to Marx, finally to the linguistic analysts.

As a result, classical political theory, with its Stoical, Christian, and juristic key-conceptions (natural law, the value of the individual, the rights of man), has died. The modern State exists not to protect our rights but to do us good or make us good—anyway, to do something to us or to make us something. Hence the new name 'leaders' for those who were once 'rulers'. We are less their subjects than their wards, pupils, or domestic animals. There is nothing left of which we can say to them, 'Mind your own business.' Our whole lives are their business.

I write 'they' because it seems childish not to recognize that actual government is and always must be oligarchical. Our effective masters must be more than one and fewer than all. But the oligarchs begin to regard us in a new way.

Here, I think, lies our real dilemma. Probably we cannot, certainly we shall not, retrace our steps. We are tamed animals (some with kind, some with cruel, masters) and should probably starve if we got out of our cage. That is one horn of the dilemma. But in an increasingly planned society, how much of what I value can survive? That is the other horn.

I believe a man is happier, and happy in a richer way, if he has 'the freeborn mind'. But I doubt whether he can have this without economic independence, which the new society is abolishing. For economic independence allows an education not controlled by Government; and in adult life it is the man who needs, and asks, nothing of Government who can criticise its acts and snap his fingers at its ideology. Read Montaigne; that's the voice of a man with his legs under his own table, eating the mutton and turnips raised on his own land. Who will talk like that when the State is everyone's schoolmaster and employer? Admittedly, when man was untamed, such liberty belonged only to the few. I know. Hence the horrible suspicion that our only choice is between societies with few freemen and societies with none.

Again, the new oligarchy must more and more base its claim to plan us on its claim to knowledge. If we are to be mothered, mother must know best. This means they must increasingly rely on the advice of scientists, till in the end the politicians proper become merely the scientists' puppets. Technocracy is the form to which a planned society must tend. Now I dread specialists in power because they are specialists speaking outside their special subjects. Let scientists tell us about sciences. But government involves questions about the good for man, and justice, and what things are worth having at what price; and on these a scientific training gives a man's opinion no added value. Let the doctor tell me I shall die unless I do so-and-so; but whether life is worth having on those terms is no more a question for him than for any other man.

Thirdly, I do not like the pretensions of Government—the grounds on which it demands my obedience—to be pitched too high. I don't like the medicine-man's magical pretensions nor the Bourbon's Divine Right. This is not solely because I disbelieve in magic and in Bossuet's Politique.[4- Jacques Benigne Bossuet, Politique tirée des propres paroles de L'Ecriture-Sainte (Paris, 1709).] I believe in God, but I detest theocracy. For every Government consists of mere men and is, strictly viewed, a makeshift; if it adds to its commands 'Thus saith the Lord', it lies, and lies dangerously.

On just the same ground I dread government in the name of science. That is how tyrannies come in. In every age the men who want us under their thumb, if they have any sense, will put forward the particular pretension which the hopes and fears of that age render most potent. They 'cash in'. It has been magic, it has been Christianity. Now it will certainly be science. Perhaps the real scientists may not think much of the tyrants' 'science'—they didn't think much of Hitler's racial theories or Stalin's biology. But they can be muzzled.

We must give full weight to Sir Charles's reminder that millions in the East are still half starved. To these my fears would seem very unimportant. A hungry man thinks about food, not freedom. We must give full weight to the claim that nothing but science, and science globally applied, and therefore unprecedented Government controls, can produce full bellies and medical care for the whole human race: nothing, in short, but a world Welfare State. It is a full admission of these truths which impresses upon me the extreme peril of humanity at present.

We have on the one hand a desperate need; hunger, sickness, and the dread of war. We have, on the other, the conception of something that might meet it: omnicompetent global technocracy. Are not these the ideal opportunity for enslavement? This is how it has entered before; a desperate need (real or apparent) in the one party, a power (real or apparent) to relieve it, in the other. In the ancient world individuals have sold themselves as slaves, in order to eat. So in society. Here is a witch-doctor who can save us from the sorcerers—a war-lord who can save us from the barbarians—a Church that can save us from Hell. Give them what they ask, give ourselves to them bound and blindfold, if only they will! Perhaps the terrible bargain will be made again. We cannot blame men for making it. We can hardly wish them not to. Yet we can hardly bear that they should.

The question about progress has become the question whether we can discover any way of submitting to the worldwide paternalism of a technocracy without losing all personal privacy and independence. Is there any possibility of getting the super Welfare State's honey and avoiding the sting?

Let us make no mistake about the sting. The Swedish sadness is only a foretaste. To live his life in his own way, to call his house his castle, to enjoy the fruits of his own labour, to educate his children as his conscience directs, to save for their prosperity after his death—these are wishes deeply ingrained in civilised man. Their realization is almost as necessary to our virtues as to our happiness. From their total frustration disastrous results both moral and psychological might follow.

All this threatens us even if the form of society which our needs point to should prove an unparalleled success. But is that certain? What assurance have we that our masters will or can keep the promise which induced us to sell ourselves? Let us not be deceived by phrases about 'Man taking charge of his own destiny'. All that can really happen is that some men will take charge of the destiny of the others. They will be simply men; none perfect; some greedy, cruel and dishonest. The more completely we are planned the more powerful they will be. Have we discovered some new reason why, this time, power should not corrupt as it has done before?

# STATISM, SECULARISM, ISLAM, AND CHRIST

### DR. JOHN M. FRAME

TODAY, CHRISTIANITY IS INVOLVED IN A GREAT CULTURAL STRUGGLE. Its two chief adversaries are secularism, the belief that society is best off without belief in God, and Islam, which believes that the God of Mohammed and the Qur'an should be supreme in every society.

Secularists often claim there are no absolutes, but in practice and often in theory they support the absolute authority of the state over all human affairs. So for them the state replaces the Christian God. This is called statism. We tend to think of statism as a modern development. Only in recent times has mankind developed sufficient technology to dream of a government that truly controls all things: witness Nazism and totalitarian Communism. But although modern technology has given a significant boost to statism, worship of the state goes back to ancient civilization. The word "totalitarianism" may be new, but the term certainly describes the root ambition of the Egyptian, Babylonian, Persian, and Roman empires, not to mention the claims of despots with merely local power.

So in the biblical period, unbelieving rulers are among the chief opponents of the kingdom of God. Satan himself is a dictator who demands that the very Son of God must bow down to him (Matt. 4:9). But all through the Bible, God's people are called to strap on their armor and to put down Satan's kingdom (Eph. 6:10-19). So in the early chapters of Genesis, God's people seek to honor God in the midst of wicked kings and kingdoms. The Pharaoh of Egypt reduces Israel to slavery, and only God's miracles set them free. In time, the empires of Assyria and Babylon take many Israelites into exile bringing great mourning until God restores them.

Jesus' disciples, as they bring the gospel to the nations, benefit from the *pax Romana*, the relative peace brought to the world by the Roman conquests. But Rome too, until its Christianization in the days of Constantine, is often an enemy of the gospel, as the Book of Revelation attests. "Jesus is Lord" (*kurios Iesous*) directly contradicted the Roman motto "Caesar is Lord" (*kurios Caesar*).

The state in itself is not a bad thing. Essentially it is a development out of the authority of the family (Ex. 20:12), attaining a level of power and complexity that the nuclear family cannot achieve, to administer justice in society. The apostles call on Christians to respect the civil magistrate and to obey it insofar as its commands do not contradict God's (Rom. 13:1-7, 1 Pet. 2:13-17). But Christians cannot accept statism, in which the state seeks to replace God as the highest authority over human life.

But secularism is meaningless unless it finds an alternative to God. The state is the most obvious candidate for such a position, for it accumulates to itself physical force, in many cases a monopoly of force. Modern technology allows states to achieve truly fearsome levels of such power. That is one basis for the state's prestige in society. Beyond that, the state is the repository of a society's values, its history, and its aspirations. So the state appropriates from its people levels of respect highly analogous to those of religion, indeed, a kind of respect more commonly given to God. So statism is typically the religion of secularism.

One might think that the state, with such power at its disposal, could leave religion alone. But as we have seen, it never does. It never regards Christianity, in particular, as an innocent societal diversion, for it understands that Christianity will not accept that status. Statists, at any rate, cannot tolerate the claim that Christ, not Caesar, is Lord.

And so it is typical of totalitarian governments to seek to destroy Christianity altogether. And even governments that are less than totalitarian find it difficult to coexist with the Christian church. The founders of the United States understood this, because the many of earliest English settlers in North America had fled religious persecution. These founders, therefore, adopted as the first amendment of the Constitution the principle of the freedom of speech and religion. Governments since then have often tried to erode this amendment by limiting its scope. The recent Affordable Care Act requires corporations to purchase insurance which covers pills thought to be abortive by many Christians. It is possible that pending lawsuits will succeed in eliminating this requirement. But resistance to it in the media and among political leaders has been muted so far. Given the language of the first amendment, one would expect an uproar against this assault on religious freedom far greater than what we have seen.

Statists have maintained that the first amendment applies only to weekly services in church buildings, so that we should speak of the freedom of worship rather than the freedom of religious practice. This is not what the first amendment says, and it is simply a denial of the freedom of religion under God. The scope of this freedom can be summarized by 1 Cor. 10:31: "whether you eat or drink, or whatever you do, do all to the glory of God." Freedom of religion must include the freedom to do all to the glory of God.[1]

It would seem that, not only Christians, but members of all religions would join this resistance to statism. Occasionally there have been flashes of such resistance, but that has been rare, so that most resistance to statism has originated among Christians. To partially explain this odd fact, let me consider more closely how Christianity differs from other faiths. My chief example will be Islam.

Islam and Christianity are similar in many ways. They both urge the worship of one God, and they both have roots in the Bible. The Qur'an, the holy book of Islam, contains many names of people familiar to Christians: Adam, Abraham, Mary, even Jesus. But in Islam, unlike Christianity, there is no distinction between church and state. For Islam, ideally, the highest religious leader is also the highest civil authority. The authority of the civil ruler is indistinguishable from the authority of God. So Islam regularly supports a kind of totalitarianism: a state that rules all aspects of human life in the name of God. In Islamic countries there is no history of free institutions, least of all freedom of religion. For this reason, I think, statists are typically much more accommodating to Islam than to Christianity. They sense that of the two, only the latter is their serious enemy.

Now totalitarianism, or at least authoritarianism, has also appeared from time to time in professedly Christian societies, such as the English society from which many of America's founders fled. But it is remarkable that Americans and others rejected this authoritarianism on premises derived from their religion. Typically, Muslims have not found justification for civil freedom in the Qur'an. But in Christian societies, the Bible has proved to be a powerful, effective means of freedom.

Americans who wish to preserve and extend political freedom, therefore, would be wise to treasure the Scriptures of the Old and New Testaments. The Scriptures are our strongest weapon against statism. And they also provide a powerful defense against the other major ideological opponent of Christianity in our time, the religion of Islam. The fight against totalitarianism is part of the Christian warfare. It is not a battle between statism and religion-in-general. It is specifically a battle between statism and Christ.

--------------------------

*About John M. Frame: John M. Frame (AB, Princeton University; BD, Westminster Theological Seminary; MA and MPhil, Yale University; DD, Belhaven College) holds the J. D. Trimble Chair of Systematic Theology and Philosophy at Reformed Theological Seminary in Orlando and is the author of many books, including the four-volume Theology of Lordship series.*

[1]Indeed, the term religion in Scripture has this broad meaning and is not limited to formal worship. See Rom. 12:1-2, James 1:26-27.

# MENE, MENE, TEKEL, UPHARSIN:

## Putting Politics into Perspective

**BY GEORGE GRANT**

POLITICS IS IMPORTANT. But it is not all-important. That is not just a modern phenomenon. It has always been a fact of life.

Many who live and die by the electoral sword will certainly be shocked to discover that most of the grand glorious headline making events in the political realm today will go down in the annals of time as mere backdrops to the real drama of everyday banalities. But it is so.

As much emphasis as is placed on campaigns, primaries, caucuses, conventions, elections, statutes, administrations, surveys, polls, trends, and policies these days, most of us know full well that the import of fellow workers, next door neighbors, close friends, and family members is actually far greater. Despite all the hype, hoopla, and hysteria of sensational turns-of-events, the affairs of ordinary people who tend their gardens and raise their children and perfect their trades and mind their businesses are, in the end, more important. Just like they always have been. Just like they always will be.

That is the great lesson of history. It is simply that ordinary people doing ordinary things are ultimately who and what determine the outcome of human events—not princes or populists issuing decrees. It is that laborers and workmen, cousins and acquaintances can upend the expectations of the brilliant and the glamorous, the expert and the meticulous. It is that simple folks doing mundane chores can literally change the course of history—because they are the stuff of which history is made. They are who and what make the world go round. As G.K. Chesterton has aptly observed, "The greatest political storm flutters only a fringe of humanity."[i]

Statism is powerful, dangerous, and nearly omnipresent in the modern world. But it is altogether out of sync with the real world and how it operates. It is not that politics is insignificant. It is just that, in the end, there are any number of things in life that are more significant.

This is the אנמ, אנמ, לקת, ויסרפו, the *Mene, Mene, Tekel, Upharsin,* the handwriting on the wall of modern statism.[ii]

Most of us would have to agree with the astute political axiom of commentator George Will, "Almost nothing is as important as almost everything in Washington is made to appear. And the importance of a Washington event is apt to be inversely proportional to the attention it receives."[iii]

Eugene McCarthy, once the darling of the New Left, also said it well, "Being in politics is like being a football coach; you have to be smart enough to understand the game, and dumb enough to think it's important."[iv]

Intuitively, we know that is true. Thus, Alexis de Tocqueville was somewhat off the mark when he asserted, "The very essence of democratic government consists in the absolute sovereignty of the majority: for there is nothing in democratic states which is capable of resisting it."[v]

Instead, we have to confess with the pundit, John Reston, that all politics is actually "based on the indifference of the majority."[vi]

According to political analyst E. J. Dionne, "Most Americans view politics with boredom and detachment. For most of us, politics is increasingly abstract, a spectator sport barely worth watching."[vii]

He says that since the average voter "believes that politics will do little to improve his life or that of his community, he votes defensively," if at all.[viii]

As odd as it may seem, that kind of robust detachment and nonchalant insouciance is actually close to what the Founding Fathers originally intended. They feared on-going political passions and thus tried to construct a non-statist system that minimized the impact of factions, parties, and activists. Citizens of the Republic were expected to turn out at the polls to vote for men of good character and broad vision—and then pretty much forget about politics until the next election.[x]

Gouverneur Morris, who actually wrote the first draft of the Constitution and was instrumental in its acceptance, said, "The Constitution is not an instrument for government to restrain the people, it is an instrument for the people to restrain the government—lest it come to dominate our lives and interests."[xi]

Similarly, Patrick Henry stated, "Liberty necessitates the diminutization of political ambition and concern. Liberty necessitates concentration on other matters than mere civil governance. Rather, whatsoever things are true, whatsoever things are honest, whatsoever things are just, whatsoever things are pure, whatsoever things are lovely, whatsoever things are of good report; if there be any virtue, and if there be any praise, freemen must think on these things."[xII]

Suspicious of professional politicians and unfettered lobbyists as well as the inevitable corruptions of courtly patronage and special interests, the Founders established a system of severe checks and balances designed to de-politicize the arena of statecraft and its attendant statesmanship.[xiii]

Though there was disagreement between Federalists and Anti-Federalists about how much "energy," or "lack thereof," government ought to exercise, there was universal agreement about what John DeWitt called the "peripheral importance of institutional action to the actual liberties of daily life."[xiv]

Thus the Founders worked together to insure that the republican confederation of states was free from ideological or partisan strife—they did everything they could to avoid the dangerous trap of statism.[xv]

Though they were not entirely successful, for much of our history American life has been marked by the distinct conviction that what goes on next door is of greater immediate concern than what goes on in Washington. Voter registration and turnout, for instance, have always been significantly lower here than in other free societies. On average, only slightly more than half of the registered voters in the United States actually make it to the polls on election day.[xvi]

Belgium, Australia, Italy, Austria, Sweden, and Iceland all average over ninety percent participation, while Canada, Japan, Britain, Germany, France, Israel, Greece, New Zealand, Luxembourg, Portugal, Spain, Denmark, the Netherlands, and Norway each see over seventy percent.[xvii]

Although there was a brief and dramatic decline in what political scientists call the "metapolitics of participation" following the presidential election of 1896,[xviii] voter turnout percentages have otherwise remained remarkably constant throughout our history.[xix]

Americans have rarely roused themselves sufficiently to get too terribly excited about their electoral choices. They generally have found something better to do than vote.

Not that any of this entirely justifies our tenured ambivalence. The fact is, at a time when statism's woes (government debt, spending, and activist intrusions into our families and communities) have grown to almost incomprehensible Babylonian proportions, our que sera sera citizenship has offered the bureaucrats and politicians in Washington tacit approval to lead us ever further down the road to ruin. And so, with Pied Piper efficiency and aplomb, they have.

During similar times of distress in our nation's history, following the Jeffersonian and Jacksonian eras, immediately after Reconstruction and the Great War, and most recently on the heels of the New Deal and Great Society episodes, Americans have stirred themselves momentarily from their laissez faire political lethargy to rekindle the fires of freedom. In the face of impending disaster, the collapse of moral resolve, the encroachment of abusive power, and the abnegation of liberty, they committed their lives and their fortunes to the process of political restoration. They proved that one of the great ironies of the American system is that there are times when politics must be treated as a matter of some-consequence so that it ceases to be treated as a matter of total-consequence.

Despite the persistent evidence that we are now living in just such a time of clear and present danger, American disinterest in politics has only ossified and hardened with the passing of time. We have yet to rally. In fact, our belligerent ambivalence over the destructive antics of politics-asusual may very well be the defining feature of our day. And to make matters worse, an oddly paralyzing sense of national malaise and a soberminded cynicism has now set in. The strange Dickensian irony is difficult to escape: these are the best of times economically but we are convinced that they are the worst of times. Despite our stunning advances and triumphs, the American people are indeed filled with uncertainty, insecurity, and dread. Polls and surveys indicate that we are fearfully gripped by a self-effacing anomie. The doom-and-gloom rhetoric of the professional socio-soothsayers has finally permeated the masses.

If things are so good then why do we think they are so bad?

The answer, according to historian Gertrude Himmelfarb, is simply that, "We think they are bad because they really are bad. Indeed, they may be worse than we think."[xx]

She says that Americans have made the startling discovery that "economic and material gains are no compensation for social and moral ills."[xxi]

Public policy scholar Os Guinness asserts, "Despite its historic political and economic triumphs, the American Republic is entering its own time of reckoning, an hour of truth that will not be delayed. It is nearing the climax of a generation-long cultural revolution, or crisis of cultural authority."[xxii]

Indeed, a veritable panoply of cultural conflicts now worry us, none of them directly related to foreign relations economic performance. The integrity of the family is sorely threatened, for instance. Educational standards seem to have utterly collapsed. Crime and violence are, in places, raging out of control. Scandal and corruption have compromised the foundational institutions of faith, politics, and charity. Racial tensions have once again erupted in our inner cities. Abortion, environmentalism, radical feminism, AIDS, pornography, drug abuse, and homosexual activism have fragmented and polarized our communities. The basic values of our nation are now persistently called into question. Patriotism has very nearly succumbed to cynicism. And in the midst of this long litany of woe, public distrust of government is epidemic — while public distrust of government officials and wanna-be government officials is pandemic.

This is the profile of that controversial and oft disputed "Culture War."[xxiii]

As Guinness has said, "Under the conditions of late modernity, the cultural authority of American beliefs, ideals, and traditions is dissolving. Tradition is softening into a selective nostalgia for the past and transcendent faiths are melting into a suburbanesque sentiment that is vulnerable to the changing fashions of the therapeutic revolution. Thus with the gravitas of their cultural authority collapsing inward like the critical mass of an exploding star, parts of American society are beginning to flare out with the dazzling but empty brilliance of a great culture in a critical phase. The result is a grand loss of confidence and dynamism. As a result of much leveling, even more unraveling, and no little reveling in both, American beliefs, ideals, and traditions are fast becoming a lost continent to many Americans."[xxiv]

Publishing mogul Malcolm Forbes says we are gripped by an "aching angst," the "social equivalent of postpartum blues."[xxv] Historian Simon Schama believes we are afflicted with "a deep and systemic sickness."[xxvi] Speech-writing wiz Peggy Noonan thinks that "the vox has popped."[xxvii] George Will says we are suffering from "a kind of slow-motion barbarization from within."[xxviii]

James Michaels summarized these provocative concerns, "It isn't the national debt or the unemployment rate or the current recession that bothers the nation's thinkers. It's not an economic mess that they see. It's a moral mess, a cultural mess. While the media natter about a need for economic change, these serious intellectuals worry about our psyches. Can the human race stand prosperity? Is the American experiment in freedom and equal opportunity morally bankrupt?"[xxix]

Political scientist James Q. Wilson says, "What frustrates many Americans, I think, is that their hardearned prosperity was supposed to produce widespread decency."[xxx]

It didn't. And as a result, we're mad.

So, what is the solution? How do we regain our bearings? It was G.K. Chesterton who first pointed the way toward a recovery from our statist stupor, "We are perpetually being told that what is wanted is a strong man who will do things" he quipped. "But, what is really wanted is a strong man who will undo things; and that will be the real test of strength."[xxxi]

Indeed, what is wanted, what is needed is an unapologetic undoing of the shallow balderdash that passes for governmental action in our day. What is wanted, what is needed is an affirmation that moral standards must undergird our society lest it collapse under the weight of our own successes. What is wanted, what is needed is a courageous harking back to the old truth that more-significant things ought to take precedence over less-significant things.

The truth is the pages of history are littered with the sad remains of mankind's glory and grandeur, grown tawdry over time. Thinking that they were in control, that they were sovereign, that they were omnipotent, even the greatest kings and tyrants, kingdoms and empires have had to face their ultimate inadequacy, mortality, and impotence. Think of Nimrod or Pharoah or Belshazzar or Caesar or Charlemagne or Napoleon for example.

Remember Nebuchadnezzar? He was the greatest king of the ancient world. His reign was resplendent with glory, honor and power. The city that he built was utterly magnificent, unrivaled in its scope and vision. The empire that he assembled was mythically proportioned, unrivaled in its strength and valor. The reputation that he forged was terrifyingly universal, unrivaled in its supremacy and vastness. And yet, Nebuchadnezzar was still but a man.

He thought he was something more. He imagined for himself a majesty that transcended that of all other men. He reveled in the storehouse of his great pride. He boasted of his invincibility.[xxxii]

But then, God humbled him. He decreed that Nebuchadnezzar would be reminded of the frailty of human flesh. He decreed that the great king would be forced to acknowledge a King greater still.[xxxiii]

The complete demise of Nebuchadnezzar was a vivid demonstration to all the citizens of Babylon that God alone is sovereign and all-mighty,[xxxiv] that God alone is exalted and praised, that God alone is the possessor of all greatness, power, glory, and majesty in heaven and on earth.[xxxvi]

The lesson was not lost on the king or his subjects:

"But at the end of that period, I, Nebuchadnezzar, raised my eyes toward heaven, and my reason returned to me, and I blessed the Most High and praised and honored Him who lives forever. For His dominion is an everlasting dominion; and His Kingdom endures from generation to generation. And all the inhabitants of the earth are counted as nothing, but He does according to His will in the host of heaven and among the inhabitants of the earth. And no one can ward off his hand or say to him: 'What hast Thou done?' At that time my reason returned to me. And my majesty and splendor were restored to me for the glory of my kingdom, and my counselors and my nobles began seeking me out; so I was reestablished in my sovereignty, and surpassing greatness was added to me. Now I, Nebuchadnezzar, praise, exalt, and honor the King of heaven, for all His works are true and His ways just, and He is able to humble those who walk in pride" (Daniel 4:34-37).

Nebuchadnezzar learned the most central truth in all the cosmos: God is God and we are not.[xxxvii] He learned that God and God alone is supreme, that God is the "King of kings and Lord of lords.[xxxix]

"The earth is the Lord's and all it contains, the world, and those who dwell in it. For He has founded it upon the seas, and established it upon the rivers" (Psalm 24:1-2).

Nebuchadnezzar had to learn the hard way that the whole universe is not man-centered—or humanistic (human=man, istic=at the center). Instead, it is God-centered—or theocentric (theos=God, centric=at the center). It is theocentric even now—despite all the sin and rebellion evident around us everywhere. God's ultimate centrality and purposeful rule is not something we must wait for. It is a reality right this very moment:

"Hallelujah! For the Lord our God, the Almighty, reigns" (Revelation 19:6).

As the Apostle Paul expressed it, the entire creation reflects the preeminence and the centrality of Christ's ongoing regency, "For by Him were all things created, that are in heaven, and that are in the earth, visible or invisible, whether they be thrones, or dominions, or principalities, or powers: all things were created by Him, and for Him: and He is before all things and by Him all things consist. And He is the head of the body, the church, who is the beginning, the firstborn from the dead; that in all things He might have the preeminence" (Colossians 1:16-18)

The Bible is absolutely clear on this point. There is nothing in heaven above or on earth below that escapes His jurisdiction. Regardless of appearances, God is God and we are not. "For the Kingdom is the Lord's, and He rules over the nations" (Psalm 22:28).

When the authority of God is no longer acknowledged in a nation, vicious spoilers rush in to fill the void. When God's sovereignty is no longer upheld in word and in deed, in spirit and in truth, petty tyrants scramble in to claim that sovereignty for themselves. They attempt to establish Nebuchadnezzar-like humanistic regimes staggering their people with the shame and humiliation that inevitably results. "Blessed is the nation whose God is the Lord" (Psalm 33:12), but woe unto those who "do not heed the works of the Lord, nor consider the deeds of His hands" (Isaiah 5:12). Through a knowledge of God's good providence "the righteous will be delivered" (Proverbs 11:9), but when there is no such knowledge "honorable men are famished the multitude is parched with thirst" and the "people go into exile" (Isaiah 5:13).

The state-sanctioned humanism that is now rapidly consuming all our hard won freedoms in America, would probably not have even been possible if Christians had not abandoned the doctrine of Christ's Lordship. If we had not shied away from a theocentric perspective of all of life, the abuses of modern American government and culture would probably never have occurred. Nearly sixty million children would never have been sacrificed on abortion's altar of lust and greed. The plague of sexual license and pornographic perversity would never have polluted our communities and neighborhoods. The attack on marriage and the family would never have been countenanced. The unabashed persecution and harassment of Christian schools and local churches would never have been sanctioned. The various agencies and functions of the federal government would never have established themselves messianically over nearly every area of life from education to aviation, from welfare to cookware, from interstate commerce to environmental protection, from land use restrictions to investment portfolio transactions. Clearly, if we are to restore our nation to sure and secure foundations we will have to do more than simply impose conservative limits on governmental jurisdiction and prerogative. We will have to admit that we ultimately must answer for our actions and inactions. We will have to reaffirm the crown-rights of King Jesus.

The handwriting is already on the wall. It is time for us to announce it to all the world just as it was so long ago to Belshazzar: *Mene, Mene, Tekel, Upharsin.*

------------------------

*George Grant, Ph.D., D.Lit., D.Hum., is the Pastor of Parish Presbyterian Church (PCA) in Franklin, Tennessee. He is the author of more than five dozen books and is the founder of Bannockburn College, Franklin Classical School, the King's Meadow Study Center, the Nuun Fund, and the Chalmers Fund.*

[i.] G.K. Chesterton, <u>G.F. Watts</u>, (New York: E.P. Dutton and Co., 1901), p. 1.

[ii.] Daniel 5:25.

[iii.] <u>Washington Post</u>, July 5, 1990.

[iv.] Jon Winokur, <u>The Portable Curmudgeon</u>, (New York: Penguin, 1987), p. 220.

[v.] Alexis de Tocqueville, <u>The Republic of the United States of America: Its Political Institutions Reviewed and Examined</u>, vol. I, (New Tork: A.S. Barnes, 1856), p. 275.

[vi.] Winokur, p. 220.

[vii. vii.] E.J. Dionne, <u>Why Americans Hate Politics</u>, (New York: Simon and Schuster, 1991), p. 9.

viii. Ibid, p. 18.

ix. Remnant Review, November 6, 1992.

x. A. James Reichley, The Life of the Parties: A History of American Political Parties, (New York: Free Press, 1992).

xi. Michael Drummond, Participatory Democracy: A New Fedralism in the Making, (New York: L.T. Carnell and Sons, 1923), p. 19.

xii. Ibid, p. 22.

xiii. Ralph Ketcham, The Anti Federalist Papers, (New York: Mentor, 1986).

xiv. Drummond, p. 17.

xv. Ross Lence, Union and Liberty: The Political Philosophy of John C. Calhoon, (Indianapolis, IN: Liberty Press, 1992).

xvi. Frances Fox Piven and Richard A. Cloward, Why Americans Don't Vote, (New York: Pantheon, 1988), p. 5.

xvii. Ibid, p. 19.

xviii. Ibid, p. 122.

xix. Ibid, p. 54.

xx. Ibid.

xxi. Ibid.

xxii. Os Guinness, The American Hour, (New York: Free Press, 1992), p.4.

xxiii. Dimensions, October 1992.

xxiv. Ibid, p. 29.

xxv. Forbes, September 14, 1992.

xxvi. Ibid.

xxvii. Ibid.

xxviii. George F. Will, Statecraft As Soulcraft, (New York: Simon and Schuster, 1984), p. 114.

xxix. Ibid.

xxx. Ibid.

xxxi. G.K. Chesterton, What I Saw In America, (New York: Dodd, Mead, and Company, 1922), p. 128.

xxxii. Daniel 4:29-32

xxxiii. Daniel 4.33

xxxiv. Revelation 17:14

xxxv. Psalm 148:13

xxxvi. 1 Chronicles 29:11

xxxvii. Psalm 103:19

xxxviii. Isaiah 40:17-18

xxxix. 1 Timothy 6:15

xl. Deuteronomy 30:17-20

xli. Deuteronomy 28:25

xlii. Isaiah 32:6-7

# SAMUEL RUTHERFORD
## and Resistance to a Tyrannical State

### BY RICHARD HANNULA

FROM THE TIME OF THE SCOTTISH REFORMATION in the 1560s, the Scots had labored to establish a national church that was independent from the crown and Presbyterian—a representative system of church government where ministers and ruling elders chosen by their congregations direct the local, regional and national courts of the church. However, maintaining the church's spiritual independence from the civil government demanded great struggle. The Stuart kings believed that they ruled by divine right—a right that included directing the governance and worship of the church. Andrew Melville, a Scottish minister and theologian, explained the distinction between church and state when he told King James VI in 1596, "Sir, there are two kings and two kingdoms in Scotland. There is King James, the head of the commonwealth; and there is Christ Jesus, the king of the church. In Christ's kingdom, you are not a king nor a lord nor a head, but a member."

James, who in 1603 became the first Stuart king to rule over both England and Scotland, would later say, "Scottish presbyterianism agrees as well with monarchy as God with the devil." When James's son, Charles I, came to the throne, interference from the crown intensified. In 1636, Charles moved to foist on the Scots an English-style episcopacy, the rule of bishops appointed by the king. A kingdom-wide crackdown on nonconformists swept up a number of the most outspoken opponents of the king's plans. Foremost among them was Samuel Rutherford. A bishops' court expelled Rutherford from his pastorate, banned him from preaching and exiled him to the far north of the kingdom.

In 1637, when King Charles I tried to force high-church worship ceremonies on the Church of Scotland, her ministers and members strongly protested the king's interference. When their repeated petitions were rebuffed, the people rose up and refused to allow the civil government to intrude in the church's worship. Charles declared all who resisted the prescribed worship rebels. Alarmed that the king's order stripped them of any legal recourse, the Scots drafted the National Covenant, pledging their loyalty to the king in his proper sphere, but promising to restore biblical worship and church government to the Church of Scotland. Tens of thousands of citizens—nobles and commoners—signed the National Covenant. Rutherford escaped his place of exile, joined the Covenanter cause and became a prominent leader in the church as they removed the king's bishops and restored presbyterian government. The church called Rutherford to be a professor of theology at St. Andrews University to train the next generation of Scottish ministers. Later, he served as a delegate to the Westminster Assembly and helped to write the *Westminster Confession of Faith.*

Over the next few years, Charles tried repeatedly to bring Scotland to heel by force of arms, but the Scots raised an army, and the Covenanter forces repulsed his efforts. Having governed without the English Parliament for most of his reign, Charles now needed it to obtain the resources that he so desperately required to deal with Scotland. The king was loathe to recall Parliament because most of its members were Puritans who shared with the Scots the same grievances against him. When the English Parliament assembled in 1640, instead of providing the king money, they demanded reforms in the English church and state. Parliament viewed the Covenanters as allies in the struggle with Charles I. This began a clash between Parliament and the king that led to civil war and Charles's downfall.

The struggle against the tyranny of Charles I prodded Rutherford to contemplate political theory. The result of his prayerful study of the

Scriptures and history was *Lex Rex*, a book about the power and place of kings and a ringing defense of constitutional government and limited monarchy. He wrote *Lex Rex* [Latin for "The Law is King"] while the civil war raged between Charles I and Parliament. The Stuart kings claimed that they answered to God alone, not to their citizens or parliaments. James VI had written, "It is treason for subjects to dispute what a king may do." On the contrary, Rutherford wrote that God entrusts earthly authority in the people and the king is empowered to work for the good of the people. Rulers receive their power from God, and the means that God uses to grant kings their authority is the consent of the people. "If he [the king] has not the consent of the people, he is a usurper,"[1] Rutherford wrote.

The people voluntarily give the king limited power to govern for their good. "They measure out, by ounce weights, so much royal power, and no more and no less,"[2] he proclaimed.

Rutherford argued that subjects were bound by the law of God to be loyal and dutiful to their monarchs. But if the king used his power arbitrarily, perverted justice and trampled the rights of elected assemblies, then, as a last resort, the people may resist their ruler by force if necessary. "Power is a birth right of the people borrowed from them," Rutherford wrote. "They may let it out for their good, and resume it when a man is drunk with it."[3]

He made it clear that citizens were not to rise up against a tyrannical king lightly or quickly. "The people are to suffer much before they resume their power,"[4] Rutherford wrote. Using many examples from the Old Testament, he supported his claim that armed defensive struggle against rulers who subvert the true faith was justified. Among the examples he cited were David resisting King Saul, and Elijah executing King Ahab's prophets of Baal. Rutherford justified armed resistance to Charles I, arguing that the king had acted unconstitutionally when he declared war against the Scots and raised an army without the consent of Parliament. Rutherford asserted that the king's actions had made him a friend of evil and "a terror to good works." He did not mince words when he recounted the violent persecution unleashed by the king who abused his power "to command an idolatrous and superstitious worship—to send an army of cutthroats against them because they refused that worship—to imprison, deprive, confine, cut the ears, split the noses and burn the faces of those who speak and preach and write the truth of God—to destroy and murder the judges of the land and the innocent defenders of the reformed religion...The man who is king, in so far as he does those things that are against his office, may be resisted."[5]

*Lex Rex*, published in London in 1644, took England and Scotland by storm. It went through multiple printings within the first few years of its release. Soon it was read throughout Europe.

When the English Parliament executed King Charles in 1649 and declared England a Commonwealth, it shook the Covenanters to the core. Although Rutherford had written against the tyranny of Charles I, he abhorred the notion that citizens would execute their own king. "Lawful resistance is one thing," he wrote, "and killing of kings is another—the one defensive and lawful, the other offensive and unlawful."[6]

In May 1660, the Commonwealth ended and the Stuart monarchy was restored when the son of the executed king was crowned King Charles II. With the collusion of impoverished Scottish nobles who did the king's bidding in Parliament in exchange for land and titles, Charles II seized nearly absolute power in Scotland. The Scottish Parliament abolished the laws supporting the independence of the church. Bishops appointed by the crown took control of the church again, and they attacked outspoken Covenanters like Rutherford. Parliament condemned *Lex Rex* as treason. A hangman burned copies of it in Edinburgh and St. Andrews. Rutherford was removed from his posts in the church and college and confined to his rooms at St. Andrews University. Not long after, Parliament sent a summons, ordering him to appear before them in Edinburgh to stand trial for high treason. When messengers delivered the summons, Rutherford was gravely ill, near death. Rutherford propped himself up in bed and said to the messengers, "Tell them that I have a summons already from a superior Judge, and I must answer my first summons; and, ere your day arrives, I will be where few kings and great folks come."

A few days later in March 1661, Samuel Rutherford died. In the ensuing years, all that had been accomplished since the Presbyterian restoration in

1637 was swept away. Constitutional barriers to ensure a limited monarchy and protect individual liberties were crippled. Covenanter ministers and members of their flocks were driven from their homes, impoverished, hunted down and slaughtered for their faith by order of the king.

But Rutherford's writings, espousing a warm and vibrant Christian life and his spirited defense of limited government, left an indelible mark on Scottish presbyterianism. In the 18th century, thousands of Scots immigrated to the American colonies, bringing their religious and political convictions with them. When the American Revolution broke out, Presbyterians played such an important role in the fight for independence that King George III referred to the conflict as the "Presbyterian War."[7] *Lex Rex* powerfully influenced the political ideas of John Locke whose writings shaped the thinking of men like Thomas Jefferson and James Madison who would author the Declaration of Independence and frame the Constitution of the United States.

----------------------------

*Richard Hannula is the principal of Covenant High School and a ruling elder in a Presbyterian Church in America congregation in Tacoma, Washington. He is the author of Samuel Rutherford: Lover of Christ; Hugh Latimer: Foremost Preacher of the English Reformation; For Christ's Crown: Sketches of Puritans and Covenanters; Radiant: 46 Remarkable Women in Church History, Our Northwest Heritage; Lights in the Northwest; and Trial and Triumph: Stories from Church History.*

[1] *Lex, Rex: or the Law and the Prince*, Samuel Rutherford, published by Robert Ogle and Oliver and Boyd, Edinburgh, 1843, p.33

[2] *Lex Rex*, p. 6

[3] *Lex Rex*, p. 123

[4] *Lex Rex*, p. 36

[5] *Lex Rex*, p.145

[6] *Lex Rex*, p. 148

[7] The Presbyterian Rebellion? Richard Gardiner, *Journal of the American Revolution*, Sept.5, 2013

# STATISM FROM AN AFRICAN PERSPECTIVE

BY NELL ROBERTSON CHINCHEN

THE BANNER BEHIND THE PLATFORM boldly declared: "If my people, who are called by my name, will humble themselves and pray and seek my face, then will I hear from heaven and will heal their land." (II Chronicles 7:14)

The president of Liberia, Dr. William R. Tolbert, had called for a National Day of Prayer. It was almost like the prophet Daniel when he read the handwriting on the wall—a fear of God hung in the air. The sins of human sacrifice, ju ju worship, and superstition were reigning and this plea was a call to repentance.

It was 1980. A short few months later, this Christian President, who was also a Baptist minister, was assassinated and the "Glorious Land of Liberty" (as sung in the Liberian National Anthem) did not long prevail. A form of Statism such as had not been seen before replaced the 150 years of Christian democracy that Liberia had enjoyed. The sovereignty of God was no longer acknowledged; the Scriptures, which had been the rule of law whereby right and wrong were decided, were disregarded. A human being in all his sin and corruption now sat on the "throne." Chaos reigned. Pandora's box of evils had been opened and the roaring lion walked about freely.

President Tolbert had tried to warn his people. The signs of Statism were like the first twinkling stars of night. The people were demanding more and more freedom from a sovereign God, not realizing they were at the same time seeking enslavement to governmental control. The first indication of this was the rice riots. Subsidy from the government was being removed from the bags of rice being sold in the capital city of Monrovia in order to encourage the farmers to go back to their villages and plant their own rice. When the people revolted and vandalized the city in protest, President Tolbert saw the prophetic handwriting on the wall.

This pressure to depend on Government rather than depend upon God would soon extend even to the churches. Persecution would come to those who refused to participate in the pagan rituals performed in the bush by the Poro and Sande secret societies. Churches were burned, men were beaten, and women were raped if they did not comply with these rules of a godless government.

Frances Shaeffer had also seen the handwriting on the wall when, 30 years earlier, he had told R. C. Sproul that his greatest concern for the churches was that they would be swallowed up by the state. No more division of church and state? In America?

Impossible! We have freedom: freedom of speech, freedom to worship, freedom to hold to our beliefs! But when these begin to be taken away, "How Then Shall We Live?" As Frances Shaeffer said so candidly.

"One nation under god, with liberty and justice for all" is what we repeat so vehemently in our Pledge of Allegiance to the American flag. But that liberty and justice only comes when that nation is "Under God", not under a sinful human being or under Statism, which leaves no room for God's inerrant Word to have authority.

"The Love of Liberty Brought Us Here", is the motto of Liberia. For 150 years there was peace. Strangely enough, when God rules a nation, there is peace. When He is taken off the throne, and man is in control, there is no peace. We watched it happen in Africa; we are watching it happen in America. It took 15 years of a brutal civil war in Liberia to reveal this truth. In America, the downward spiral has been slower. It is almost as though America has turned into the citizens of Sleepy Hollow. ("The Legend of Sleepy Hollow" by Washington Irving, written in 1820) Or, maybe, as one who had been a prisoner of war during World War II traveled about America upon his return home and seeing Communism encroaching on the shores of America, shouted, 'AMERICA, DON'T YOU CARE?" This he repeated over and over in his speeches—over and over as he traversed this vast nation: 'AMERICA, DON'T YOU CARE?" No one heeded his warning. No one really cared.

How can you listen, anyway, with the sounds of the world pounding in your ears? And who cares who is at the helm of the ship steering that vessel wherever he desires as long as it doesn't affect me personally. WHO CARES?

The clarion call to stand against the insidious onslaught of Statism is subtle. There seems to be a hesitancy to shout as did Paul Revere when he made that daring midnight ride: "Wake up! The British are coming! Wake up"! There was a passion then to fight for the birth of a "new nation under God, which could long endure." There are no brave men on horseback today to cry out the warning to "beware! You are losing the freedom you fought so hard to obtain!"

Sadly, warnings are not heeded until the danger comes closer to home. We were in Liberia in March, 2014, when the Ebola epidemic first broke out in the country of Guinea, which bordered the city of Yekepa, where the African Bible College is located. The border was immediately closed. Outside the country of Liberia, however, no one really cared.

Even the people in the villages, who had no knowledge of its danger, did not seem to care. When a group of concerned individuals, including a pastor, journalists, and health workers, tried to bring them the information on how to be protected from this deadly disease, they killed eight of them with machetes and threw their bodies in the nearest latrine. Sort of a reminder of the parable Jesus told in Mark 12:1-12.

We realized then how vital was the radio station on the African Bible College campus. The borders may be closed, but the airwaves are open! The warnings could be heard by all who would listen. Not only could the message be sent out on how to be saved from the plague of Ebola but we could also send out the message of salvation. People will listen because now the danger lurks at their doorstep.

The eminent danger of Statism is no longer just an idle threat. Even as the Ebola epidemic was ignored until it crossed the border into America, so this philosophy of Statism, much like that of Communism, Nazism, Radicalism, and Socialism, can no longer be ignored.

C.S. Lewis, in his article, "Mere Liberty and the Evils of Statism," (published in three parts) clearly shows that he is diametrically opposed to governmental control. This is further demonstrated by his refusal to be knighted by Winston Churchill in 1951 as "Commander of the Order of the British Empire." Even the characters in his books, *The Screwtape Letters* and *The Chronicles of Narnia* are examples of those seeking to cast off the chains of government.

I will go one step further. I believe Statism has caused the moral compass of our country to go haywire. If we wonder what has happened to bring about this moral relativism we need only to look at the leadership of our nation.

John C. Calhoun (who was raised a strict Calvinist), in his paper, "A Disquisition on God" dated 1848 (Notes on John C. Calhoun, published by Liberal Arts Press, N.Y. 1953) asks a key question: "How can those who are invested with the powers of government be prevented from employing them as the means of aggrandizing themselves instead of using them to protect and preserve society?" (271-272)

The answer to that question is only if that ruler is subject to the Laws of God himself will he be able to use his power to protect those who are under his authority, and ONLY if he himself upholds the moral guidelines of God's Holy Word will he be able to impart those values to his people. And yet, for years in my Genesis classes at the African Bible Colleges in Liberia and Malawi and over the four African Bible College Radio stations, I have emphatically stated: "God uses sin as a stepping stone to accomplish His purposes." This is clearly demonstrated throughout the Book of Genesis but especially in the life of Joseph. As he said to his brothers, "As for you, you meant it for evil against me, but God meant it for good." (Genesis 50:20)

In his article entitled "God Glorified In the Evils of Statism," C. Jay Engels uses the first published sermon by Jonathan Edwards (1731) entitled, "God Glorified in Man's Dependence" to clarify this statement:

> "God is glorified in the evils of Statism because the Christian notes this despicable world is not his permanent residence. It is in times of prosperity and earthly freedom that we become complacent and comfortable in the very lives which we are to see as temporary. In times of comfort, we forget that we are not supposed to focus on storing up our treasures here on this earth. We should rather, as citizens of God's heavenly kingdom, focus on our long-term investment. That is, our eternal investment. Nothing that we do here will be beneficial here in the long run. All that is eternally good, is eternally good precisely because it will be fulfilled after this world passes away. We recognize that we are pilgrims on this journey and we live life in light of eternity. And the first step of being a disciple of God is recognizing that eternity matters far more than temporary things. Under the tyrannies of Nero, the Christian church was purified, made strong, and declared that God eternal was the very source of all that was good, despite the evils of Rome's Statism. In making a commitment to eternity, God is glorified."

This is exactly what happened in Uganda. The ruthless ruler Idi Amin so persecuted the people, and especially the Christians, that the Church became strong and steadfast to the principles of God's Holy Word. It is still so today. The Anglican Church has refused to bend to the pressure from the leaders of America to relinquish these beliefs. God has been glorified.

We know that "God sets up one and puts down another." As Jesus said to Pilate, "You would have no power at all against me except it were given you from above." (John 19:11a) Nevertheless, God allows corrupt, oppressive leaders to rule with the hope that men would turn in desperation to see His Grace. It is this dependence upon our Holy God that brings glory to Himself.

The chains of Tribalism that prevailed in Liberia for hundreds of years were only broken when the freed slaves (many from the state of Mississippi) landed on its shores with the hope of bringing the Gospel to those were lost. Christianity was quickly accepted by those hungry people who lived along the shores of Liberia. But those who attempted to penetrate the dark interior of the thickest forest in all of Africa found that the barriers of disease, witchcraft and superstition soon dispelled this eagerness to take the Gospel to the uttermost parts of the world. (Mark 16:15)

Slowly, this difficult challenge was accomplished, however. Brave missionaries began to push through these obstacles and churches were established in the interior of Liberia; schools were started, mission stations, small clinics, leprosy colonies begun - all with the purpose of teaching and preaching God's Word.

The Tribalism - much the same as our Statism in America - remained, even though Christianity was strong and prevalent. After the brutal fifteen years of Civil War, we soon realized that syncretism, however, had so invaded the churches that it was difficult to differentiate between the two.

Man, by God's divine decree, is given the choice. His elect but need to be obedient to His standards of conduct, and to reject those who would rule over him who are not "under God's authority'.

Wake up! You residents of Sleepy Hollow; "Be on the alert!" as shouted Paul Revere; "America- Don't you care?"

Democracy cannot exist unless God is sovereign, unless the Bible is the "only rule of faith and practice." May God's people no longer be deceived by the empty promises of Statism, but may we stand once again upon the faithful promises of our God and King.

-----------------------------

*Nell Robertson Chinchen, Co-Founder, African Bible College*

# STATISM, REAGAN, AND RELIGIOUS LIBERTY

### BY MICHAEL A. MILTON

THE POSTMODERN LANDSCAPE OF THE WEST has been scorched by the unforgiving fires of secularism. Aleksandr Solzhenitsyn (1918-2008) wrote of its desolate wasteland. He had seen it in the Soviet gulag[1] only to see its hideous and dark spirit appear in late twentieth century America and Britain:

**"The entire twentieth century is being sucked into the vortex of atheism and self-destruction. We can only reach with determination for the warm hand of God, which we have so rashly and self-confidently pushed away... There is nothing else to cling to in the landslide."[2]**

As we wind our way through the early years of the twenty first century the secular state seems to grow unabated and many fear that the landslide is inevitably leading to disaster. It is dangerous to ever disagree with Solzhenitsyn, but I do think there is something to cling to in the landslide. There is, of course, as the great Russian freedom man reminded us, hope in the very God we deny. Time and time again, He has proven that His love and grace are greater than all our disregard. Yet we must first *remember* Him, as Aleksandr Solzhenitsyn reminded us in his Templeton Prize speech in 1983. But speaking of those instruments that God has provided for us, signposts to His grace, if you will, I think that we, also, have the legacy of the 40th President of the United States to hold onto. I believe that President Ronald Reagan's legacy of religious liberty is, indeed, a strong branch to hold onto in the secular landslide and spiritual erosion of our own day. Let me explain what I mean, briefly, by pointing to two enduring areas of Ronald Reagan's legacy that help us today to strengthen our grip on religious liberty and thus have the optimism and hope that President Reagan had against all odds.

**First, President Reagan's Legacy of Religious Liberty is that Religious Liberty is the First Right of all Rights.**

We all know that President Reagan often used the John Winthrop phrase "city on a hill" phrase taken from his sermon[3] aboard the Pilgrim ship *Arbela*, sailing to America from England. The phrase became the very hallmark of President Reagan's political vision of America's past and America's future. [4][5] It was a vision grounded in his understanding of the American dream. America was a nation of men and women who had covenanted with God to do great things for others if God would give His blessing to them and their posterity. President Reagan believed that we lived on the spiritual capital of those prayers and promises. He once said,

**"While never willing to bow to a tyrant, our forefathers were always willing to get to their knees before God. When catastrophe threatened, they turned to God for deliverance."** [6]

We need to remember that we don't live in a secular state. We live in a nation where the government was guarded from meddling with the free expression of worship of a faithful people. This is the first clause of the first amendment of the Bill of Rights. For President Reagan, it was first in his life also.

In his first year in office, during his first Christmas address to the nation, the President took the opportunity to share his own faith with the nation. Ronald Reagan knew that he was addressing a nation filled with a host of people expressing their faith in many ways, as it should be in America. Yet as president he modeled that one did not have to leave faith at the door just because you worked in a government building. So he shared his faith that the child in the manger born that night was more than a baby. He believed that He was the Lord. The Washington Post printed the President's address, but did not print that part of his address. President Reagan's pastor at National Presbyterian Church in Washington D.C., The Reverend John Boyles, was flabbergasted.[7] He wrote to the Washington Post to protest what they had done. Nothing happened. So the pastor printed the entire address in the church bulletin. He was surprised when the received a note from President Reagan thanking him for printing his address, including his testimony about Jesus Christ. Having recently transferred his membership into the church from Bel Air Presbyterian Church in California, President Reagan added in the hand written note that he wanted never to embarrass the pastor or congregation or let them down. The pastor could not believe that the POTUS was reading the church newsletter! Yet it revealed what President Reagan felt was of supreme importance: religious liberty.

He would later demonstrate this in his dealings with Mikhail Gorbachev and with other world leaders.[8][9] He would prove this with seeking the asylum of Jews who wanted to leave the Soviet Union to immigrate to Israel. He would prove it in his support of Roman Catholics in Eastern Europe.[10]

And this is what we learn: we must not muzzle anyone of any faith, including evangelical Christianity and conservative Jews and Roman Catholics who so often do get muzzled. If those, whose voices represent the main voices of freedom in Western Democracy are shut up, then other religions will soon be silenced as well. Islam flourished here because Christianity and Judaism is strong. If the faith of the Bible on which Western Civilization is silenced, then all faiths, and those of no faiths, will be subject to harassment or worse.

Religious Liberty is the first right of all rights. That is the first legacy lesson of President Reagan. The second is like unto the first.

**President Reagan's Legacy of Religious Liberty is that Religious Liberty is Fundamental to all other Rights.**

This is very close to the first legacy lesson, but it is somewhat different. What does it mean that religious liberty is fundamental to all other rights? It means that when the founders placed religious liberty as the first of all of the Bill of Rights, the other rights derived their existence from this right. Freedom of conscience in expressing faith in the world towards the ultimate questions of a Creator, of the existential questions of "Who am I? Why am I here? And Where am I going? What is life all about?" gives worth and value to what it is to be human. If that is taken away, then all other rights are lost. As President Reagan put it in his address to a prayer breakfast in 1984,

**"Without God, there is no virtue, because there's no prompting of the conscience....Without God, there is a coarsening of the society. And without God, democracy will not and cannot long endure."**[11]

The only president to write a book on the value of human life in the womb was Ronald Wilson Reagan. In his classic book, *Abortion and the Conscience of a Nation*, President Reagan wrote,

**"Despite the formidable obstacles before us, we must not lose heart. This is not the first time our country has been divided by a Supreme Court decision that denied the value of certain human lives. The Dred Scott Decision of 1857 was not overturned in a day, or a year, or even a decade" (p. 19).**[12]

In that book, Reagan also wrote,

**"The question today is not when human life begins, but, *What is the value of human life*? The abortionist who reassembles the arms and legs of a tiny baby to make sure all its parts have been torn from its mother's body can hardly doubt whether it is a human being."**[13]

We live in a day when *Statism* is replacing our dependence upon self, the family, the community, the Church and synagogue, the grassroots government systems, and in many cases, God.

**"Statism is the belief that the civil government (or man via simple government) is the ultimate authority in the earth and as such is the source of law, moral righteousness (that which is right and wrong). Statism is a religious belief. Socialism may be a mild form of statism, but it is rooted in the same non-biblical presuppositions."**[14]

Statism is the apocryphal beast-like power that whispers in Eden, "Did God really say?" Statism is that diabolical voice which speaks through the earthly powers that chafe under the authority of God, "Why do the heathen rage, and the people imagine a vain thing? The kings of the earth set themselves, and the rulers take counsel together, against the Lord, and against his anointed, saying, Let us break their bands asunder, and cast away their cords from us" (Psalm 2:1-3 KJV). Statism is the spirit of wickedness from below that causes persecution of religion, suppression of thought, and will be the culmination of all past and present evil systems of government that opposes the things of God when, at length, the mysterious will of the Almighty is fulfilled and the ravenous beast is destroyed after this "little" season of frantic usurping the King. Until then, all faithful people must beware of any attempt to gather absolute power away from themselves into a collective where human pride and weakness may be subject to the overwhelming seductive forces of a tyrannical Statism. For the spirit of the Evil One first devours a man's soul before it devours others. The spirit of Statism inhabits a "carrier" whose own life has been made susceptible to the evil entry through his or her own wounds or failures. Then, having secured a suitable "host," the despicable pathogen's poison spreads until there is a sufficient power base to trap and destroy its prey, always the lives of human beings and always their inalienable rights being the choicest and first targets. Yet Statism offers great gifts and promises of security for those who will yield their liberty to the collective without a fight. Healthcare, education, in a word—cradle to grave care by the Collective—for absolute support of the Collective insures your security and your family's security. The trade off is simply, sadly, heretically, and, inhumanly, your soul.

This is Statism and its dangers to the human spirit and to our lives today are as real as when Diocletian persecuted the Church in Rome in the early Fourth Century or when the Soviet Union persecuted the Russian Jews in the Twentieth Century.

It is no wonder, then, that the State seems to march unimpeded through increasing layers of our lives. There seems to be a veritable welcome mat at so many front doors. But there is a Faustian deal and a devil's debt to be paid for trading our freedom for security from the government. It was a deal that President Reagan warned us against. The deal usually involves the taking of religious liberties first because the State, a beast-like force that is operated by an elite hierarchy, sometimes unwittingly doing the bidding of unseen powers, strikes first at the fundamental of all rights, religious liberty, in order to deal a blow to all liberties. Reagan knew this. The city on a hill reminded him of the fundamental nature of that liberty. That city must continue to shine in our own commitments and we must never allow her gates to be opened to any who would offer us safety if we just stop letting the light shine for just one second. It is, as the President would say, still the last best hope for mankind.[15]

In 2004, Jerry Newcombe interviewed Dr. Paul Kengor for a TV piece on President Reagan's faith.[16] Dr. Kengor said, "What the historical record has overlooked is that Ronald Reagan was carried by a set of Christian convictions that go back to the 1920's that carried him even longer, and that, in fact, informed those political convictions that came later. And that's the side of Ronald Reagan that we all missed."

I happened to believe that the famous Reagan optimism is grounded in the faith of Ronald Reagan, a faith that grew stronger through the years. Ronald Reagan believed that only one thing could ever hurt this nation and that would be if we finally forget that we really were the city on the hill that Winthrop prayed for us to be on that ship in the Atlantic ocean that day. If religious liberty, the first of all liberties, the fundamental liberty that feeds freedom itself, were taken for granted, then we would lose the connection with the One who has secured the blessings of freedom for America. In days like these it is good that we recall these prophetic words from President Reagan: **"If we ever forget that we're one nation under God, then we will be a nation gone under."**[17]

I don't believe we are there. I believe that there are still many who pray for God to stir our hearts to seek His face and turn to Him for guidance in these days. Amidst all of the social engineering that the current administration is doing with our military I still see soldiers turning to God. As a Christian minister I still pray with soldiers to receive Christ. I still lead people in prayer in civic gatherings in our country. I still see the expressions of faith that are present in the many immigrants coming to our shores. America is not forgetting God even if some in our government may be and some elites may want us to. The problems are too great. The challenges of life are too complicated. The landslide is happening too quickly.

But there is something to hold onto. There is a legacy. There is a city on a hill still shining. Thank God. And thank God that every now and then He exalts righteousness in our midst and gives us a leader who reminds us that the city is not made with human hands, but is an eternal city that we seek. I can think of no more powerful words in this regard than words Ronald Reagan declared when asked about the greatest need of our nation. His reply?

**"I think our nation and the world need a spiritual revival as it has never been needed before ... a simple answer ... a profound and complete solution to all the trouble we face."[18]**

I hope you will allow me the license at a time like this to say "Amen." For the sake of all men and women of all faiths I pray that too. May God bless you and may God bless America with such vision again. Thank you.

-------------------------

*Michael A. Milton, Ph.D. (University of Wales, Trinity Saint David's College) is a Presbyterian minister (PCA), educator, author, public servant, and musician. The president of Faith for Living, Inc. and the D. James Kennedy Institute, he is the speaker on the national broadcast, Truth that Transforms*

[This is adapted from an address that was given at the Ronald Reagan Ranch Center in Santa Barbara, California on Thursday, September 26, 2013.]

[1] Solzhenitsyn, Aleksandr. *The Gulag Archipelago, 1918-1956: An Experiment in Literary Investigation I-IV; Translated from the Russian by Thomas P. Whitney.* Collins, Fontana, 1976.

[2] "Men Have Forgotten God" – The Templeton Address. (September 1983). Retrieved March 29, 2014, from http://www.roca.org/OA/36/36h.htm.

[3] Winthrop, John. "A modell of Christian charity." *Winthrop Papers* 2 (1994): 1929-47.

[4] See Jones, John M, and Robert C Rowland. "A Covenant-affirming jeremiad: The post-presidential

ideological appeals of Ronald Wilson Reagan." *Communication Studies* 56.2 (2005): 157-174.

5. Reagan, Ronald. "We Will Be A City Upon a Hill." *Speech to the First Conservative Political Action Conference* 25 Jan. 1974.

6. Ronald Reagan: Proclamation 4897 - *National Day of Prayer*. (March 19, 1981). Retrieved March 29, 2014, from http://www.presidency.ucsb.edu/ws/?pid=42169.

7. Listen to Reverend Boyles' narration of this entire event at Paul Kengor, ed. The 7th Annual Ronald Reagan Lecture: "God and Ronald Reagan, Revisited". *The Center for Vision and Values Ronald Reagan Lectures*. February 5, 2013. Grove City College, 2013. Proceeding.

8. Jones, John M, and Robert C Rowland. "Reagan at Moscow State University: Consubstantiality Underlying Conflict." *Rhetoric & Public Affairs* 10.1 (2007): 77-106.

9. Farr, Thomas F. *World of faith and freedom: why international religious liberty is vital to American national security*. Oxford University Press, 2008.

10. Kengor, Paul. *The crusader: Ronald Reagan and the fall of Communism*. Reagan Books, 2006.

11. "Remarks at an Ecumenical Prayer Breakfast in Dallas, Texas." *Remarks at an Ecumenical Prayer Breakfast in Dallas, Texas*. 23 August 1984. Web. 30 Mar. 2014. <http://www.reagan.utexas.edu/archives/speeches/1984/82384a.htm>.

12. Reagan, Ronald Wilson. *Abortion and the Conscience of the Nation*. Nashville: Nelson, 1984. 22. Print.

13. See Judge William P. Clark's article in the New York Times: William P. Clark, "For Reagan, All Life Was Sacred." *The New York Times*. The New York Times, 10 June 2004. Web. 31 Mar. 2014. <http://www.nytimes.com/2004/06/11/opinion/for-reagan-all-life-was-sacred.html>.

14. Stephen McDowell. *Rendering to Caesar the Things That Are God's: Statism: The Golden Calf of the Modern World*. 1st ed. Vol. 23. Charlottesville, VA: Providence Foundation Biblical Worldview University, 2009. 15. Print. Providence Perspective Ser.

15. Ronald Reagan. *Speaking my mind: Selected speeches*. Simon and Schuster, 2004.

16. TruthinAction.org.

17. Reagan, Ronald W. "Remarks at an Ecumenical Prayer Breakfast in Dallas, Texas." Remarks at an Ecumenical Prayer Breakfast in Dallas, Texas. University of Texas Archives, 23 Aug. 1984. Web. 30 Mar. 2014. <http://www.reagan.utexas.edu/archives/speeches/1984/82384a.htm>.

# 'STATISM' AND THE UK

## BY MOSTYN ROBERTS

THE HORSE IN THE FABLE was desperately seeking help against the stag. He asked the man for assistance. The man mounted him. The stag was defeated. But the man would not get off. The horse's ally had become his master.

People look to the state for help. As we shall see later there are various reasons for this in the UK but the fact is that it has become a habit. Christians share this habit. It is not a total surprise then when the one to whom we look for help turns on us and starts pushing us around.

The welfare state benefits system, education, the National Health Service – all provide services and resources for what many would regard as the necessities of life. As one born in Britain in the 1950s I have benefitted enormously from these provisions. I do not think it wrong that a government should provide for the poor. How though can one do that without creating a consumer, even a victim, mentality in the population at large?

All this has been without any major *conscious* ideological shift in British thinking. We have not had a political revolution, we have not officially become communists. What has undoubtedly happened is that a creeping socialism has taken over the major political parties so that some commentators lament that all a Conservative government does is cement the last batch of socialism and indeed introduce some more. Some argue that there is no longer a truly 'conservative' party in the UK – without doubt one of the reasons for the rise of UKIP (the United Kingdom Independence party, formed to get Britain out of the European Union but now taking on a major protest role in British politics).

More socialist, generally, than the major parties on the national (UK) stage are the nationalist parties of Wales and Scotland and the representatives of the national parties who sit in the devolved assemblies in those nations/regions. One of the most startling manifestations of 'Gov-max' has been the proposal in Scotland in the Children and Young People (Scotland) Act 2014 to assign to every child under the age of 18 in Scotland a state-employed Named Person who would be able to share information with a wide range of public authorities. This may be well-intentioned, to protect vulnerable children before the event of abuse or neglect kicks in. But it looks awfully like the nanny state taken to the nth degree, an 'ultimate insult' to every loving parent, a message that the state knows best, a 'decisive battle in the war against parents', as it has been called; parents cannot be trusted to raise their own children. Not surprisingly, attempts to implement this proposal have met with opposition on the ground.

There are certainly those who have written, schemed and worked for centralised government but what we have in the UK is a kind of 'creeping statism' not by diktat or by ideological decree but by a combination of public sloth and self-indulgence. People do not consciously invest the British government with supreme authority, but in practice we have grown used to the state providing for us from the cradle to the grave, and quite honestly, we rather enjoy it. This is Aldous Huxley's *Brave New World* more than George Orwell's *1984*. We are trapped more by what we enjoy than by the violence of an oppressor. We invited the man to get on our back and now he won't get off. As C.S. Lewis said in his 1958 essay *Willing Slaves of the Welfare State*, "The modern State exists not to protect our rights but to do us good or make us good - anyway, to do something to us or to make us something. Hence the new name 'leaders' for those who were once 'rulers'. We are less their subjects than their wards, pupils, or domestic animals. There is nothing left of which we can say to them, 'Mind your own business.' Our whole lives are their business."

That is what we (Christians included) seem to want. Until it restricts our freedoms.

## RENDER UNTO CAESAR...
In replying to the scribes and the chief priests Jesus made a distinction between what is owed to the state and what is owed to God: 'render to Caesar the things that are Caesar's, and to God the things that are God's.' (Luke 20:25). It is clear from this and from Paul's teaching in Romans 13:1-7 that the state has a legitimate claim on the Christian's obedience. This however is not an absolute claim. To 'honour the emperor' appropriately is to recognise him as appointed by God so that in 'rendering unto Caesar' we are in fact obeying God, not just Caesar.

Statism is what happens when the state sees itself as autonomous, or people attribute autonomy to it, or in practice regard it as autonomous. How has this happened in Britain over the last sixty or so years?

### 1. The impact of socialism
As outlined above, this is a major ideological change in Britain over the last three generations. There is much that is good in it. I believe it is part of the duty of a government to provide for the poor and those who cannot help themselves. This has good biblical precedent in the legislation of ancient Israel. The notion of an individual providing entirely for himself can be as much of an idol as the nanny state. Yet combined with secularism it has produced a dependent mentality where personal responsibility gives way to receiving handouts, the provision of mercy is seen to be a right and the paternalism of the state takes over from the Fatherhood of God as the ultimate provider. The real issue I believe is the spiritual decay of the nation, not the policies of socialism in themselves.

### 2. The culture of 'Gov-max'
There is something bizarre about the Prime Minister being asked for his opinion when an author says something apparently rude about Princess Kate

(the wife of Prince William); or sending a telegram of congratulation to the first gay couple to marry under new legislation. National leaders are under pressure either from journalists, or from their own perception as to what will pay off politically, to express their opinion on all manner of events that in the past might have been called trivial. Partly this is the influence of the media which like a magnifying glass makes government seem even bigger than it is; partly to the celebrity culture which gives undue attention to matters which are not much better than gossip; and to the chattering classes which, like 'twitter' and the Athenians, 'spend their time in nothing except telling or hearing something new' (Acts 17:21).

All this has the effect of promoting politicians into the headlines whether they like it or not. Nothing can happen, even if it has nothing to do with the politician's job, without the Leader being asked what he thinks about it, or volunteering his view. Inevitably government is seen as 'big' and as intruding into all areas of life.

## 3. The shrinking of God
'We don't do God' famously said a press officer of Tony Blair, a former Prime Minister. That would not have gone down well in the USA, one suspects. It is no doubt in some ways very English. Religion and death (and once, sex) were things you did not talk about at the dinner table and certainly not if they became personal in any way. But the comment is also symptomatic of the increasing secularism of the country. God is reduced to the realm of the private – as R.C. Sproul says, Christians can practise their religion rather like native Americans used to be expected to restrict their culture to the reservations. Just don't bother anyone else with it!

The privatisation of religion and the exclusion of Christianity from 'the public square' in the west has been widely noted and needs no further discussion here.

## 4. False reliance on an established church
Unlike the USA, there is the establishment of religion in the UK in the form of the Church of England. Superficially one might have expected this to make 'doing God' more, not less, common in public. However it is a fact of history that the nation with a constitutional prohibition on the establish-

ment of religion (famously if not entirely accurately paraphrased as ' the separation of church and state') is more influenced by Christianity in its public life than the country that has had an established church for five and a half centuries. The reasons for this are complex but it certainly cannot be asserted that the established church has successfully upheld Christian values in British politics. The undoubted and foundational Christian influence in the constitution and laws of this country, from Alfred the Great in the ninth century onwards, are due to godly men in high places, widespread Reformation and revival and the work of the Spirit and the Word rather than to the impact of the religious establishment as establishment. In 2013 fifteen of twenty-four bishops in the House of Lords abstained in the vote on same sex marriage. It is perhaps not being too judgmental to see this as symptomatic of how the established church has been sucked in to the secular system.

A sad feature of the establishment of religion, despite the fine Reformed foundation documents of the Church of England, a history of great men and women and wonderful works of God done in and through it, is that it contributes in no small measure to the deceit that Britain is a 'Christian country'. If being a Christian country means that Christian values are deeply embedded in the laws and morality and values of the nation, then Britain could be called a 'Christian country', but it is questionable how much, as I have said above, that is due to the established church as such. What establishment does do unfortunately is cause people to think that because they are born in Britain they are Christians (though that idea is certainly diminishing now); that a parish is the community of God's people so that many Anglican clergymen see little need to have a strong theology of conversion; and (perhaps worst of all) that we should be shoring up the establishment to protect the Christian faith and morals. Even evangelical non-conformists today, under the pressures of secularism, relativism, the 'gay' lobby and Islam can seem too concerned about propping up a 'Christian' establishment as if that were part of building the kingdom of God. We seem to have lost touch with our roots which were in the separation of church and state.

## 5. The unwelcome uncle
There is a palpable hostility to Christianity in the popular media. This is true on a national and local level. The Christian voice is not one people want to

hear. Christians are given a rough time, as if the Christian faith was a cause of embarrassment, like an eccentric uncle at a party you wish would go away, and even of evils, rather than a source of blessing. Since the recent atrocities in Pakistan and Paris, Muslims have been given air-time to explain that these appalling acts of terrorism were 'not really Islamic'. Had such acts been committed by Christian extremists (and of course the telling fact is that such an act would be exceptional), one wonders if Christians would have been given the same indulgence to provide an apologia for the faith.

## 6. The blunderbuss effect

The blunderbuss was a type of firearm which, instead of firing one bullet more or less accurately, scattered pellets over a wide are. Such is the effect of actions taken to restrain terrorists. Because of the actions of a few, everyone has to undergo security checks. The relatively quiet English village in which I live, about twenty miles north of London, has four security cameras to survey one short and very quiet high street. Britain has more CCTV cameras than any other nation in Europe. Peace and security are prioritized over freedom.

Equality of course is an overriding principle. Because of the importance of being seen to be fair and treating all sides equally, counter-terrorist measures in response to Muslim extremism are restricting civil freedoms. Homosexuals are a particularly protected minority. Many street evangelists and preachers have run into difficulty with police in recent years for teaching the Bible's view on this issue, often getting provoked into saying something which can then be labelled 'offensive'. In a number of cases the police have had to back down when they realised that no crime has been committed. But it shows the official mindset.

Thankfully legislation which made it possible for people to be arrested for saying something which 'insulted' others has been curtailed; the government was also blocked in 2014 from outlawing people doing something 'annoying' in public. However they plan to bring in a law enabling police to restrict 'harmful activities' by what are called Extremist Disruption Orders. The practice of penalising people before they had committed a crime began many years ago with ASBOs (Anti-Social Behaviour Orders). Anti-social behaviour is a positively Orwellian label for anything a government, or local police officer, does not like. But that is the way things are going. All this is justified with the best of intentions - security and peace trump all.

## A SPIRITUAL ISSUE

The American situation, of course, is serious too. Prominent in our press has been the case of the pastors in Houston, Texas ordered to hand over any materials in which they had said anything against homosexuality, equal rights legislation or the lesbian mayor. Even a written constitution, as decisions of the Supreme Court since *Roe v Wade* (1973) have revealed, are not proof against secularism in the mindset of the public, politicians and the judiciary. The majority of Christians it appears think that being Republican, or in the UK Conservative, might just mean the rot has not gone quite so far, but that is not saying much; the present Conservative government has been one of the most morally liberal, but in terms of liberty of conscience and religion, most oppressive, governments in modern history. That it is a coalition (with the Liberal Democrats) makes little difference – Prime Minister David Cameron has recently said, without coalition pressure, that the same sex marriage legislation has been the proudest achievement of his time in office.

So we are foolish if we think this is a political issue. By all means let Christians get involved in politics; let us campaign against unrighteous laws; let us pray for those in authority; speak out and fight for what we believe in the forthcoming UK general election. I am not advocating retreating into a ghetto and doing nothing but evangelise. The fact remains however that unless there is a major turning of hearts back to the Lord and his laws, the only way our nation can go is downhill. The economy is going up (slowly) but then, so was that of Israel in the generation or two before God sent in the Assyrians. As Schaeffer often repeated, if there is no God (which there is not, in practical terms, in the thinking of the vast number of people in the west), anything is possible. He was more far-sighted than many in seeing that if God is rejected, tyranny is not just a possibility, it is mathematically certain. The only viable long-term option to statism is Christian theism. If God is not boss, man will be. If His Word is not our authority, man's must be. If man is not honoured as created in the image of God, society will be fair game for any despot. If the Triune God is not the basis of harmonising the one and the many, unity and diversity, form and freedom, then the only way to prevent anarchy is tyranny.

The issue is profoundly spiritual.

Mostyn Roberts.

------------------------

*Mostyn Roberts is the pastor of Welwyn Evangelical Church in Hertfordshire. After reading law at Pembroke College, Cambridge he practiced as a solicitor for seven years. He responded to the call to the ministry, taking a BA at Spurgeon's College in London followed by the MTh at the University of London. After a pastorate in the north of England he came to Welwyn at the end of 1998. He has taught Systematic Theology at LTS since 2002.*

# "SEMPER FI!"

### BY D. JAMES KENNEDY

*"Fear none of those things which thou shalt suffer: behold,*
*the devil shall cast some of you into prison, that ye may be tried;*
*and ye shall have tribulation ten days: be thou faithful unto death,*
*and I will give thee a crown of life."*

REVELATION 2:10

IT WAS NIGHTTIME WHEN WE LANDED at the airport, and a deep darkness hung over the countryside. The stars glittered with unusual brightness in a moonless sky. We were excited, my wife Anne and I, as we got into a cab to make our way into the city of Izmir. The city was located on the opposite side of a bay from the airport, so we drove around the bay. The night was windless, as well, and the water was as smooth as a black mirror.

The city of Izmir, located on a high hill, was scintillating with brilliant lights, which were reflected perfectly off the black surface of the water beneath. It was, without any doubt, we both agreed, the most magnificent approach to any city I have ever visited—and I have visited a lot of cities. Izmir, where we had come to in a brief flight from Istanbul, is located about twenty miles north of the city of Ephesus, in what was once Asia Minor, but now is Turkey. It is, of course, the modern name for the ancient city of Smyrna. One of the letters Christ wrote to the seven churches that are included in the second and third chapters of the book of Revelation was written to the church at Smyrna.

Toward the end of that letter there is the famous statement from Christ where He says, "Be thou faithful unto death, and I will give thee a crown of life" (Revelation 2:10). It is a glorious text. It can be seen imbedded magnificently in the marble floor just inside the front door of this church.

The reason for my preaching on this text today is because a number of things have come to my mind and heart in recent weeks that have weighed heavily upon me, and that I believe we need to consider seriously. I was reading recently about an author of many books, who naturally had thesauri which contain, of course, thousands of quotations from hundreds and hundreds of various authors. Recently he bought three new ones, and he said he was amazed when he looked up the term "honor," "faithfulness," and found that there were no quotes by any modern author at all included in any one of these three newly printed thesauri.

Strange, I thought. Then I read elsewhere that a survey of high school seniors revealed that very few of them knew what the English word "fidelity" meant, but a large number of them— tragically and ironically—knew what the word "infidelity" meant. Maybe they heard the word used in regard to their parents' divorce. It seems that the concepts of fidelity, honor and loyalty are disappearing from our culture.

This was not true, however, in Smyrna. In the centuries before Christ, Smyrna had become a Roman colony. They were noted for their faithfulness, for their fidelity to the Empire and to the Caesar. When other cities were attempting to secede, when treachery and conspiracies were abounding, when wars were raging around them, the city of Smyrna remained ever faithful. In the first century A.D., when Christ was brought by the apostle to the city of Smyrna, many came to know the Savior, and they, too, were known as "faithful" Christians.

So we have this encouragement from Christ, **"Be thou faithful unto death, and I will give thee a crown of life."** I hope that verse is imprinted in your mind and that you will remember it and reflect on it often.

They were faithful Christians. In fact, the bishop at the Smyrna church when these words were written by John, was a disciple of John's, one of his converts. His name was Polycarp, one of the famous church fathers in the second century who became a martyr for Christ.

I remember, when I was a new Christian I didn't know that much about the historical evidences that so clearly confirm and establish the Christian faith as real and historical and accurate. I must confess that the devil placed in my mind several times the doubt, "I wonder if this could all have happened on a cloud somewhere in somebody's imagination? I wonder if this is really historical at all?"

Then I came across a book containing the letters of Polycarp, who lived in the first and second centuries. He is not part of the biblical records, but he did write many letters. I was thrilled when I discovered conversations he had had with the apostle John:

- How they had walked along the seashore and John had told him about the times he had walked along another seashore with Jesus Christ,
- and of the teachings of the Savior and how he had heard the music of His voice and felt the magic of His personality,
- and how His life had been transformed by Christ,
- and how he had stood at the foot of the cross at Calvary and heard the final words of Christ before He expired.

Through Polycarp, this whole Christian truth was brought down and it was nailed into the bedrock of history for me. My faith was strengthened by him, and I want to thank him someday when I see him in heaven. Polycarp was brought to trial when he was eighty-six years old. He said that as a child and through all of his life he had followed Christ, and Christ had never failed him. He had ever been faithful. How could he deny Him now? And Polycarp was martyred for his faith and received that crown of life.

But the church at Smyrna remained faithful, even after the onslaught of Islam, when thousands of Muslims began to migrate from North Africa and Saudi Arabia into Asia Minor (now Turkey) trying to take over all of Europe. The Christians at Smyrna remained firm and resisted that onslaught until 1424. Smyrna was the last city in Asia Minor to finally yield to that onslaught. They were faithful unto death.

Why is my message titled "Semper Fi"? Do you know what that means? If you served in the United States Marine Corps you know, for it is the motto of the United States Marines.

Now they are a glorious corps. They are older than the United States. They were formed by the Continental Congress in 1775, before the Constitution, before the U.S. government, before the American Revolution, and they have fought in every war the United States has ever been in. Truly, as the Marine hymn puts it, "From the halls of Montezuma to the shores of Tripoli, we will fight our country's battles on the land and on the sea." And then, somewhat good naturedly, "If the army and the navy ever look on heaven's scenes, they will find the streets are guarded by the United States Marines."

Though such high-spirited words encourage and lift the spirits of would-be marines, I am afraid that is not theologically sound. With ten thousand times ten thousand angels, there is really no need for marines to guard heaven's streets. Not only that, there is nothing to guard the streets from! There will be no thieves, robbers, murderers, or villains of any kind on the streets of heaven because all of Christ's enemies will have been cast into outer darkness and will never be heard from again. But we understand the sentiment that is expressed.

## ALWAYS FAITHFUL
Semper Fi, the shortened form of semper fidelis, means "always faithful." And I will say, and you think about it, the United States Marines, though not a group of angels, have done extraordinarily well in exemplifying that motto for well over 200 years. For the entire history of the United States, from Guadalcanal to Okinawa, and all of the rest of the places where the marines have landed, the U.S. has been victorious.

What about you? Are you always faithful? Are you always faithful to Jesus Christ? Another reason I am preaching this text, for those who have grown up in the last thirty-five years or so and have been a part of the "me" generation, there is no doubt that this concept, as well as these words, are truly foreign to your vocabulary. If you are part of the "me" generation, and if you are looking out for number "1" and putting number "1" first, you are not faithful to anyone but yourself.

With all apologies to the Bard of Avon, if you are true only to yourself, it is not possible that you can be true to anybody else. Sadly, we have seen this decline in fidelity, in faithfulness, in loyalty, and in honor in our country in the last few decades

- Many people today are not faithful to their spouses.
- We have the worst divorce record in the world.
- They are not faithful to their churches.
- They are not faithful to Christ.
- They are not faithful to their country.

They are just always unfaithful. You can count on it, pretty much, and that is a tragic and sad commentary about our nation and the days in which we live.

Jesus was the ever-faithful, semper fidelis man. The book of Revelation says, **"He that sat upon him** [the white horse] **was called Faithful"** (Revelation 19:11). And His followers, are described as **"they that are with him are called, and chosen, and faithful"** (17:14).

Faithful, of course, means "full of faith." There are people today who are faithful; they are faithful to their own selves. They are faithful to their own bank accounts. They are faithful to their own advancement. They are faithful to themselves and nothing else. They are faithful to their quest for pleasure, but they are not faithful to Christ and His Church. They are not serving Him faithfully, as the United States Marines have served their country through their corps.

We should be faithful to Christ and serve Him through His Church. We are called to be soldiers of Christ. We are called to endure hardness for His sake.

We are told and admonished by Christ: **"Be thou faithful unto death and, I will give thee a crown of life"**—not a miserable half-living existence, like many people eke out in this world filled with sorrows, and pains, and aches, and heartaches, and heartbreaks, and finally, death. But He promises a glorious, everlasting, never-ending imperishable life in paradise in a body that will never grow old, will never get arthritis, will never ever die. Christ says, "I will give them the crown of an imperishable and never-ending life."

To whom will He give this gift? To those who are faithful. Note well: we are not saved by our own doing. We are saved by faith in the faithful One who is Christ, because none of us, if the truth is really known, are semper fi. We are more or less faithful, at best. But Christ is the everfaithful One, and when we take hold of Him by faith, His faithfulness flows into us. Therefore, one of the inevitable qualities of those who are connected to Christ by faith is that they are filled with faith. They are faithful unto death.

The sufferings I mentioned earlier—with Polycarp—were prevalent in the first three centuries of the Roman persecution. Ten huge tidal waves of persecution swept across the Roman Empire, from Nero to Diocletian, rising with an ever-greater crescendo of fury. The most horrific, terrible, unbelievable tortures that only the most depraved of minds could conceive of were inflicted on Christians.

That persecution did not end in the third century, but it goes on through the centuries. Amazing to tell, mirabile dictu, in the twentieth century there have been more martyrs for Christ than in any other century, including the first. Millions upon millions of Christians have been found "faithful unto death" in this century. The Chinese, in the Cultural Revolution, killed every Christian they could get their hands on. The Koreans in North Korea took whole bodies of Christians, marched them onto bridges and pushed them off into freezing water amidst the ice to freeze and drown.

## FAITHFUL UNTO DEATH

So it has been, and so it is. I recently returned from Washington to be a part of the first-ever conference to endeavor to bring an end to, or at least ameliorate, the terrible persecution of Christians going on around the world—to bring the influence of the United States government to bear upon these nations which are persecuting Christians, many of which enjoy "most favored nation" status with the United States.

Our vacillating, spineless, faithless State Department, at least many of its members, was very outraged when the Saudi Arabians wanted to close the nightclub and end the worship services we had there for Americans. They put up such a strong fight for the nightclub that it is still open. The churches they allowed to be closed.

It is outrageous the way our government and our State Department have often refused to even listen to the stories of Christians who have been persecuted in other countries but, instead, they give them back to their persecutors to be killed. The U.S. government's influence brought an end to the persecution of Jews in the Soviet Union. It could also bring an end to the persecution of Christians in most of the nations of the world, as well.

In a church, I believe it was in Sudan, government troops swept down upon a small congregation and took them into prison. They were tortured by their Muslim captors, but they let the pastor go free. Wasn't that gracious. Just let him go. They said, "There's the door. Go on out." But first they pulled his eyes out! Then, with blood streaming down his face from his eyeless sockets, he staggered blindly down the road as an object lesson to other Christians as to what would happen to them.

In Sudan, for just coming into a worship service you could be taken outside and nailed to a tree. Many Christians in this past year have been crucified in Sudan. And our government has said nary a mumbling word about it. We're going to change that.

Are you faithful unto death? Salvation is through faith in Jesus Christ, but our faithfulness is the only way we can reveal the reality of that faith. Am I a Christian? Are you? The only way you can know I am a Christian—that I have faith, and am filled with faith—is that I am faithful.

Dear ones, I am worried about some of you. I do not see faithful service to Christ in the core of His Church—the soldiers of Christ. I do not see you serving Him. I believe some of you lied when you sang "I love to tell the story, for some have never heard." I don't believe it. You haven't told that story to anybody in the last year, have you? Some of you have never told that story to anybody in your entire lifetime. You are not faithful! **"Be thou faithful unto death, and I will give thee a crown of life."**

I remember a story about a small church out in the boonies of the Soviet Union in their heyday. In the midst of a service attended by about a hundred people, suddenly there was a crash, as four soldiers kicked in the front door and stomped down to the front of the church with machine guns turned on the congregation. They said, "You filthy Christians. You are the offscouring of the earth. You are a plague on the glorious atheistic society of the Soviet Union and you are going to die today. You are not fit to live. You are a blotch on our glorious motherland. However, there may be some among you who are not here because you believe this foolish nonsense, and we will give you one minute to get out of this building."

Silence. Then suddenly the scuffle of feet, and about half the congregation raced for the door, after which one soldier closed it. The others with their machine guns trained on the congregation set them down and said, "Brethren, we have come to worship Christ with you, but first we had to get rid of the hypocrites." What about you? Would you be in or out of that church? "Be thou faithful unto death, and I will give thee a crown of life." Death? Life! The promise of Him who is Life itself. Ah, dear ones, how our nation, how our church needs faithful ones. I hope that this day many of you will commit your lives, or commit them afresh, to be faithful unto Christ and you will take for your own the motto of the United States Marines: Semper Fi, "ever faithful, O Christ, my King."

*****

**PRAYER:** Lord, forgive us for our infidelity, for our unfaithfulness, for our lack of service, for our presumption that because we have made a profession of faith and attend the weekly service that we are soldiers of Thine. We have been unfaithful in so many things. We do not serve Thee, we do not witness to Thee, we do not give as we should, we do not tell the story. We offer Thee not one hour of service. We have been almost ever unfaithful. O God, we repent while yet there is time, that we might be among those faithful ones who shall wear upon their heads the crown of life and be the recipients of that gift of a never-ending, imperishable, glorious eternal life which Thou wilt give unto them who are faithful unto death. In Thy name, O Christ, our King, we pray. Amen

--------------------------

*Dennis James Kennedy (November 3, 1930 – September 5, 2007), better known as D. James Kennedy, was an American pastor, evangelist, and Christian broadcaster. He founded the Coral Ridge Presbyterian Church in Fort Lauderdale, Florida, where he was senior pastor from 1960 until his death in 2007. Kennedy also founded Evangelism Explosion International, Coral Ridge Ministries (since 2011, Truth in Action Ministries), the Westminster Academy in Fort Lauderdale, and Knox Theological Seminary.*

[Sermon delivered by Dr. D. James Kennedy on January 28, 1996, at Coral Ridge Presbyterian Church in Fort Lauderdale, Florida]

# THE ESSENCE OF LIBERALISM

## BY JERRY NEWCOMBE
6/10/14

As the fallout from the Bowe Bergdahl swap for five Taliban prisoners of war continues to reverberate, there's a fascinating statement from one MSN-BC host on the subject.

On 6/4/14, "Now with Alexander Wagner," the MSNBC host said she hoped the swap may lead to "broader negotiations" with the Taliban. (Hat tip to newsbusters.org).

"Broader negotiations" with the terroristic Taliban? Reasoning with those who have proven themselves incapable of humane reasoning?

This got me to thinking: What is the essence of liberalism? Is it elitism---the notion that big government can take better care of you and yours than you can?

Is the essence of liberalism the abolition of private property? Is it that people should have the freedom to do whatever they want to, to define their own right and wrong?

I think all these things are corollaries, no doubt. But in my view the essence of liberalism begins with a flawed premise, a flawed anthropology, that says that man is basically good.

In the liberal view, we can negotiate with the Taliban, even though they want to kill us unless we convert to their brand of Islam, because deep down they're good.

In 1938, British Prime Minister Neville Chamberlain could proudly declare there will be "peace in our time" because he had the signature of "Herr Hitler" to prove it. Subsequent events in World War II proved him stupendously wrong.

The problem of liberalism is that it doesn't recognize the biblical truth, proven repeatedly in history, that man is sinful and that the best form of government recognizes that and therefore separates power, so no individual or oligarchy can amass too much of it.

Why has America historically succeeded in granting us freedom? It's because the founding fathers recognized this fact. They did everything in their power to limit how much power any one man or group of people might have.

James Madison played an important role in the writing of our Constitution. He noted that since men are not angels, government is necessary. But men are not angels, and since government is run by men, we also need protection from the government (Federalist #51). Belief in the sinfulness of man can be seen in the Constitution with its strict separation of powers.

The Bible is very clear. It does not teach that we are perfect, but rather that we are sinful. Jesus said, "If you then, who are evil…" Paul said, "There's no one good, no, not one." Jeremiah noted, "The heart is deceitful above all things, and desperately sick; who can understand it?"

Mankind tends toward evil. Therefore, power must be separated. I am not aware of a single example of any of the founders of America believing that man was basically good. This is not cynical. It's just the reality and has led to the most prosperous forms of government—and economics too.

Like the other founders, Thomas Jefferson said that power should be divided for everybody's sake: "The way to have good and safe government is not to trust it all to one, but to divide it among the many..." No phone and pen there.

James Madison said, "All men having power ought not to be trusted."

Ben Franklin said, "There is scarce a king in a hundred who would not, if he could, follow the example of Pharaoh, get first all the peoples' money, then all their lands and then make them and their children servants forever."

Alexander Hamilton wrote, "Til the millennium [when Jesus reigns on earth] comes, in spite of all our boasted light and purification, hypocrisy and treachery will continue to be the most successful commodities in the political market."

In the early 20th century, Christian apologist G.K. Chesterton once wrote a letter to his newspaper on "what's wrong with the world." His essay was only two words: "I am."

There's a link between correct anthropology and good government. Those governments, like that of the U.S. (as the founders envisioned it), have given freedom because the founders acknowledged man's corrupt nature.

In contrast, the former Soviet Union, as an opposite example, built their system of government on an atheistic, Marxist base—on the notion that man is basically good, but corrupted by capitalism and religion. Marx thought when the workers seized the means of production and the reins of government and imposed the worker state, then government would become unnecessary and wither away.

So the new Soviet man or woman was to be free from religious superstitions and from the curse of selfishness as found in capitalism with its emphasis on private property. Who created a better system? The communists or America's founders? The answer is obvious.

Historian Paul Johnson said the 20th century state, in large part because of communism (which asserted the basic goodness of humanity) has proven to be the greatest killer of all time.

No wonder God sent a Savior to save us from our sins. Meanwhile, deals should take into consideration man's nature as it really is, and not as it should be in someone's playbook.

----------------------------

*Dr. Jerry Newcombe is a TV producer and the cohost of Kennedy Classics. He has written/co-written 24 books, including The Book that Made America (on the Bible) and (with Dr. Kennedy) What If Jesus Had Never Been Born? and (with Peter Lillback), George Washington's Sacred Fire. He hosts gracenetradio.com Thurs-noon (EDT). tiam.org@newcombejerry*

# Introduction to
# SILENT NO MORE

## BY DOUGLAS KELLY

MICHAEL MILTON HAS ACCURATELY DIAGNOSED the potentially fatal disease that is so painfully eating out the vitals of our Western culture. The outward manifestation of that dread disease is *statism*, and it is a malignant (and understandable) response to the moral relativism that has resulted from the West's rejection of the truth of God and the salvation it sets forth.

No normal being would enjoy being told by the doctor that tests indicate that he or she has cancer, *unless* the indications are that it has been discovered in time for appropriate medical treatment to cure it. That is precisely the twofold function of *Silent No More*: it looks beneath the surface of the skin to find out what is the nature of the underlying disease that is inexorably taking away the life of our political culture and normal society, and in so doing it provides us bright and realistic hope of a profound cure and restoration to health (painful and disturbing though it may be), insofar as we humble ourselves to seek the healing grace of God so freely offered to us in the Gospel of Christ. Dr. Milton cannot, and wisely does not, predict whether our increasingly secularist society will ever bow the knee to the only One who can forgive and restore it, but those of us who know him cannot doubt the direction in which he is praying!

Major revivals are always unlikely, yet in the good providence of God they do break out with beneficent and transforming effects when least expected. Sometimes a humble and massive turning back to God may be related to a truer vision of where the church and country are and precisely what has gone wrong for them to have fallen into the filthy pit. I pray that Mike Milton's book may serve such a function. It is written in clear English, and in terms that ordinary people in today's society can make sense of. At times it is uncomfortable, like some of the diagnostic procedures of a good doctor. It is not afraid to discuss controversial matters that will not be acceptable to the politically correct hand that weighs so heavily on our contemporary public discourse. Although parts of it will be annoying to some, it will make others cry out with insight: 'Now I see, and now I know what must be done!'

A great value of this book is that it helps us grasp the parts in light of the whole; that is, it sheds much light on the confusing attacks that seem to keep coming every day in politics, education, the arts and the media, against the largely Christian way of life that many of us were raised in. There is a fullness and wholeness about this little volume, so that it does not leave us mounting a constant, tiresome, knee-jerk reaction against horrendous trends that keep washing against us like the waves of the incoming tide of the sea. I think its diagnosis enables the interested reader to make sense of the whole thing that is really happening that otherwise could overwhelm us with a plethora of depressing details. 'Yes,' we may say, ' we have grasped what is really wrong; we can make enough sense of it to begin taking action, that will –with the help of the sovereign and gracious God of Holy Scripture – lead to a multitude of healings and restorations that may surpass our fondest dreams of revival and renewal.'

Dr. Milton will show you that statism essentially replaces worship in and obedience to the Triune God, with trust in and submission to the national state (or international world order). In the mentality of statism, all problems are basically caused by the central state not having enough power ceded to it. The solution is always a larger, stronger state, which requires withdrawing liberty from the churches, the local regions, and the family. The USSR that finally collapsed between 1989 and 1991 showed in flesh and blood where statism leads mighty nations. Siberia and other camps of the Gulag Archpelago, so terrifyingly described by Solzenitsyn are the end results of faith in the omnicompetent state. Yet that fall, and the human grief and unspeakable loss that lay behind it, seem not to have been seriously noticed by the majority of our Western intelligentsia, who are crying out for the same kind of statist control twenty years after Russia collapsed from within.

Why would very intelligent people try to repeat such disastrous historical experiments that have woefully failed in the recent past? Here is the reason, and you will find it in the pages of Dr. Milton's volume: when we turn our hearts away from God, we inevitably turn to something else to replace him. (The Apostle Paul discusses this same reaction in Romans, chapter 1). The Triune God is, generally in European and American thought since the 18th century Enlightenment, replaced by the central state, which the famous 19th century German philosopher Hegel famously termed 'God walking on earth.'

A Europe (soon followed by America), that wanted to get rid of the Triune God with his 'repressive moral code' and his unwelcome Lordship over its life, had to reject his written Word, and to replace that Word with something else in order to do so. In most cases it started with lifting up various shapes of humanist philosophy above a discredited Holy Scripture, and this secularist philosophy then became the basis of legislative enactments, quite contrary to the divinely revealed moral code. An illustration would be the 1973 'Roe v. Wade' decision of the US Supreme Court, which 'legalizes' that which God strictly forbids humans to do: the taking of innocent life of the unborn. And more recently we see legislative actions seeking to allow homosexual unions, in face of the prohibition of such things by God's written Word, and by the consensus of nearly every nation for millennia. Such are the results of the cancer of willful spiritual blindness (to what God says in his Word and in also our own conscience, as we see in Romans chapter 2), and its never-failing offspring: moral relativism. Spiritual blindness to the true structure of human life and society always results in more potent statism, which exacerbates the underlying disease. The Fall of the Berlin Wall and of the Soviet Union show us what will happen in due season, unless we go in a different direction.

*Silent No More* will show you that infinitely better way, if, by the grace of God, you are interested. I pray that you will be! No matter how dark our day may be, in terms of II Chronicles 7:14, I consider it definitely not too late for revival and renewal. This book could help push us in that direction, and that is why Michael Milton wrote it.

---------------------------

*Douglas Kelly, Ph.D., James Jordan Chair of Systematic Theology, Reformed Theological Seminary, Charlotte, NC*

# "A TIME FOR CHOOSING"

## (The Speech)

## 1964

**BY RONALD REAGAN**

*A Time for Choosing, also known as The Speech, was a speech presented during the 1964 U.S. presidential election campaign by future president Ronald Reagan on behalf of Republican candidate Barry Goldwater. It is considered the event that launched Reagan's political career.*

THANK YOU. Thank you very much. Thank you and good evening. The sponsor has been identified, but unlike most television programs, the performer hasn't been provided with a script. As a matter of fact, I have been permitted to choose my own words and discuss my own ideas regarding the choice that we face in the next few weeks.

I have spent most of my life as a Democrat. I recently have seen fit to follow another course. I believe that the issues confronting us cross party lines. Now, one side in this campaign has been telling us that the issues of this election are the maintenance of peace and prosperity. The line has been used, "We've never had it so good."

But I have an uncomfortable feeling that this prosperity isn't something on which we can base our hopes for the future. No nation in history has ever survived a tax burden that reached a third of its national income. Today, 37 cents out of every dollar earned in this country is the tax collector's share, and yet our government continues to spend 17 million dollars a day more than the government takes in. We haven't balanced our budget 28 out of the last 34 years. We've raised our debt limit three times in the last twelve months, and now our national debt is one and a half times bigger than all the combined debts of all the nations of the world. We have 15 billion dollars in gold in our treasury; we don't own an ounce. Foreign dollar claims are 27.3 billion dollars. And we've just had announced that the dollar of 1939 will now purchase 45 cents in its total value.

As for the peace that we would preserve, I wonder who among us would like to approach the wife or mother whose husband or son has died in South Vietnam and ask them if they think this is a peace that should be maintained indefinitely. Do they mean peace, or do they mean we just want to be left in peace? There can be no real peace while one American is dying some place in the world for the rest of us. We're at war with the most dangerous enemy that has ever faced mankind in his long climb from the swamp to the stars, and it's been said if we lose that war, and in so doing lose this way of freedom of ours, history will record with the greatest astonishment that those who had the most to lose did the least to prevent its happening. Well I think it's time we ask ourselves if we still know the freedoms that were intended for us by the Founding Fathers.

Not too long ago, two friends of mine were talking to a Cuban refugee, a businessman who had escaped from Castro, and in the midst of his story one of my friends turned to the other and said, "We don't know how lucky we are." And the Cuban stopped and said, "How lucky you are? I had some-place to escape to." And in that sentence he told us the entire story. If we lose freedom here, there's no place to escape to. This is the last stand on earth.

And this idea that government is beholden to the people, that it has no other source of power except the sovereign people, is still the newest and the most unique idea in all the long history of man's relation to man.

This is the issue of this election: Whether we believe in our capacity for self-government or whether we abandon the American revolution and confess that a little intellectual elite in a far-distant capitol can plan our lives for us better than we can plan them ourselves.

You and I are told increasingly we have to choose between a left or right. Well I'd like to suggest there is no such thing as a left or right. There's only an up or down—[up] man's old—old-aged dream, the ultimate in individual freedom consistent with law and order, or down to the ant heap of totalitarianism. And regardless of their sincerity, their humanitarian motives, those who would trade our freedom for security have embarked on this downward course.

In this vote-harvesting time, they use terms like the "Great Society," or as we were told a few days ago by the President, we must accept a greater government activity in the affairs of the people. But they've been a little more explicit in the past and among themselves; and all of the things I now will quote have appeared in print. These are not Republican accusations. For example, they have voices that say, "The cold war will end through our acceptance of a not undemocratic socialism." Another voice says, "The profit motive has become outmoded. It must be replaced by the incentives of the welfare state." Or, "Our traditional system of individual freedom is incapable of solving the complex problems of the 20th century." Senator Fullbright has said at Stanford University that the Constitution is outmoded. He referred to the President as "our moral teacher and our leader," and he says he is "hobbled in his task by the restrictions of power imposed on him by this antiquated document." He must "be freed," so that he "can do for us" what he knows "is best." And Senator Clark of Pennsylvania, another articulate spokesman, defines liberalism as "meeting the material needs of the masses through the full power of centralized government."

Well, I, for one, resent it when a representative of the people refers to you and me, the free men and women of this country, as "the masses." This is a term we haven't applied to ourselves in America. But beyond that, "the full power of centralized government"—this was the very thing the Founding Fathers sought to minimize. They knew that governments don't control things. A government can't control the economy without controlling people. And they know when a government sets out to do that, it must use force and coercion to achieve its purpose. They also knew, those Founding Fathers, that outside of its legitimate functions, government does nothing as well or as economically as the private sector of the economy.

Now, we have no better example of this than government's involvement in the farm economy over the last 30 years. Since 1955, the cost of this program has nearly doubled. One-fourth of farming in America is responsible for 85 percent of the farm surplus. Three-fourths of farming is out on the free market and has known a 21 percent increase in the per capita consumption of all its produce. You see, that one-fourth of farming—that's regulated and controlled by the federal government. In the last three years we've spent 43 dollars in the feed grain program for every dollar bushel of corn we don't grow.

Senator Humphrey last week charged that Barry Goldwater, as President, would seek to eliminate farmers. He should do his homework a little better, because he'll find out that we've had a decline of 5 million in the farm population under these government programs. He'll also find that the Democratic administration has sought to get from Congress [an] extension of the farm program to include that three-fourths that is now free. He'll find that they've also asked for the right to imprison farmers who wouldn't keep books as prescribed by the federal government. The Secretary of Agriculture asked for the right to seize farms through condemnation and resell them to other individuals. And contained in that same program was a provision that would have allowed the federal government to remove 2 million farmers from the soil.

At the same time, there's been an increase in the Department of Agriculture employees. There's now one for every 30 farms in the United States, and still they can't tell us how 66 shiploads of grain headed for Austria disappeared without a trace and Billie Sol Estes never left shore.

Every responsible farmer and farm organization has repeatedly asked the government to free the farm economy, but how—who are farmers to know what's best for them? The wheat farmers voted against a wheat program. The government passed it anyway. Now the price of bread goes up; the price of wheat to the farmer goes down.

Meanwhile, back in the city, under urban renewal the assault on freedom carries on. Private property rights [are] so diluted that public interest is almost anything a few government planners decide it should be. In a program that takes from the needy and gives to the greedy, we see such spectacles as in Cleveland, Ohio, a million-and-a-half-dollar building completed only three years ago must be destroyed to make way for what government officials call a "more compatible use of the land." The President tells us he's now going to start building public housing units in the thousands, where heretofore we've only built them in the hundreds. But FHA [Federal Housing Authority] and the Veterans Administration tell us they have 120,000 housing units they've taken back through mortgage foreclosure. For three decades, we've sought to solve the problems of unemployment through government planning, and the more the plans fail, the more the planners plan. The latest is the Area Redevelopment Agency.

They've just declared Rice County, Kansas, a depressed area. Rice County, Kansas, has two hundred oil wells, and the 14,000 people there have over 30 million dollars on deposit in personal savings in their banks. And when the government tells you you're depressed, lie down and be depressed.

We have so many people who can't see a fat man standing beside a thin one without coming to the conclusion the fat man got that way by taking advantage of the thin one. So they're going to solve all the problems of human misery through government and government planning. Well, now, if government planning and welfare had the answer—and they've had almost 30 years of it—shouldn't we expect government to read the score to us once in a while? Shouldn't they be telling us about the decline each year in the number of people needing help? The reduction in the need for public housing?

But the reverse is true. Each year the need grows greater; the program grows greater. We were told four years ago that 17 million people went to bed hungry each night. Well that was probably true. They were all on a diet. But now we're told that 9.3 million families in this country are poverty-stricken on the basis of earning less than 3,000 dollars a year. Welfare spending [is] 10 times greater than in the dark depths of the Depression. We're spending 45 billion dollars on welfare. Now do a little arithmetic, and you'll find that if we divided the 45 billion dollars up equally among those 9 million poor families, we'd be able to give each family 4,600 dollars a year. And this added to their present income should eliminate poverty. Direct aid to the poor, however, is only running only about 600 dollars per family. It would seem that someplace there must be some overhead.

Now—so now we declare "war on poverty," or "You, too, can be a Bobby Baker." Now do they honestly expect us to believe that if we add 1 billion dollars to the 45 billion we're spending, one more program to the 30-odd we have—and remember, this new program doesn't replace any, it just duplicates existing programs—do they believe that poverty is suddenly going to disappear by magic? Well, in all fairness I should explain there is one part of the new program that isn't duplicated. This is the youth feature. We're now going to solve the dropout problem, juvenile delinquency, by reinstituting something like the old CCC camps [Civilian Conservation Corps], and we're going to put our young people in these camps. But again we do some arithmetic, and we find that we're going to spend each year just on room and board for each young person we help 4,700 dollars a year. We can send them to Harvard for 2,700! Course, don't get me wrong. I'm not suggesting Harvard is the answer to juvenile delinquency.

But seriously, what are we doing to those we seek to help? Not too long ago, a judge called me here in Los Angeles. He told me of a young woman who'd come before him for a divorce. She had six children, was pregnant with her seventh. Under his questioning, she revealed her husband was a laborer earning 250 dollars a month. She wanted a divorce to get an 80 dollar raise. She's eligible for 330 dollars a month in the Aid to Dependent Children Program. She got the idea from two women in her neighborhood who'd already done that very thing.

Yet anytime you and I question the schemes of the do-gooders, we're denounced as being against their humanitarian goals. They say we're always "against" things—we're never "for" anything.

Well, the trouble with our liberal friends is not that they're ignorant; it's just that they know so much that isn't so.

Now—we're for a provision that destitution should not follow unemploy-ment by reason of old age, and to that end we've accepted Social Security as a step toward meeting the problem.

But we're against those entrusted with this program when they practice de-ception regarding its fiscal shortcomings, when they charge that any criti-cism of the program means that we want to end payments to those people who depend on them for a livelihood. They've called it "insurance" to us in a hundred million pieces of literature. But then they appeared before the Su-preme Court and they testified it was a welfare program. They only use the term "insurance" to sell it to the people. And they said Social Security dues are a tax for the general use of the government, and the government has used that tax. There is no fund, because Robert Byers, the actuarial head, appeared before a congressional committee and admitted that Social Security as of this moment is 298 billion dollars in the hole. But he said there should be no cause for worry because as long as they have the power to tax, they could always take away from the people whatever they needed to bail them out of trouble. And they're doing just that.

A young man, 21 years of age, working at an average salary—his Social Se-curity contribution would, in the open market, buy him an insurance policy that would guarantee 220 dollars a month at age 65. The government promis-es 127. He could live it up until he's 31 and then take out a policy that would pay more than Social Security. Now are we so lacking in business sense that we can't put this program on a sound basis, so that people who do require those payments will find they can get them when they're due—that the cup-board isn't bare?

Barry Goldwater thinks we can.

At the same time, can't we introduce voluntary features that would permit a citizen who can do better on his own to be excused upon presentation of evidence that he had made provision for the non-earning years? Should we not allow a widow with children to work, and not lose the benefits suppos-edly paid for by her deceased husband? Shouldn't you and I be allowed to declare who our beneficiaries will be under this program, which we cannot do? I think we're for telling our senior citizens that no one in this country should be denied medical care because of a lack of funds. But I think we're against forcing all citizens, regardless of need, into a compulsory government program, especially when we have such examples, as was announced last week, when France admitted that their Medicare program is now bankrupt. They've come to the end of the road.

In addition, was Barry Goldwater so irresponsible when he suggested that our government give up its program of deliberate, planned inflation, so that when you do get your Social Security pension, a dollar will buy a dollar's worth, and not 45 cents worth?

I think we're for an international organization, where the nations of the world can seek peace. But I think we're against subordinating American interests to an organization that has become so structurally unsound that today you can muster a two-thirds vote on the floor of the General Assembly among nations that represent less than 10 percent of the world's population. I think we're against the hypocrisy of assailing our allies because here and there they cling to a colony, while we engage in a conspiracy of silence and never open our mouths about the millions of people enslaved in the Soviet colonies in the satellite nations.

I think we're for aiding our allies by sharing of our material blessings with those nations which share in our fundamental beliefs, but we're against doling out money government to government, creating bureaucracy, if not socialism, all over the world. We set out to help 19 countries. We're helping 107. We've spent 146 billion dollars. With that money, we bought a 2 million dollar yacht for Haile Selassie. We bought dress suits for Greek undertakers, extra wives for Kenya[n] government officials. We bought a thousand TV sets for a place where they have no electricity. In the last six years, 52 nations have bought 7 billion dollars worth of our gold, and all 52 are receiving foreign aid from this country.

No government ever voluntarily reduces itself in size. So governments' programs, once launched, never disappear.

Actually, a government bureau is the nearest thing to eternal life we'll ever see on this earth.

Federal employees—federal employees number two and a half million; and federal, state, and local, one out of six of the nation's work force employed by government. These proliferating bureaus with their thousands of regulations have cost us many of our constitutional safeguards. How many of us realize that today federal agents can invade a man's property without a warrant? They can impose a fine without a formal hearing, let alone a trial by jury? And they can seize and sell his property at auction to enforce the payment of that fine. In Chico County, Arkansas, James Wier over-planted his rice allotment. The government obtained a 17,000 dollar judgment. And a U.S. marshal sold his 960-acre farm at auction. The government said it was necessary as a warning to others to make the system work.

Last February 19th at the University of Minnesota, Norman Thomas, six-times candidate for President on the Socialist Party ticket, said, "If Barry Goldwater became President, he would stop the advance of socialism in the United States." I think that's exactly what he will do.

But as a former Democrat, I can tell you Norman Thomas isn't the only man who has drawn this parallel to socialism with the present administration, because back in 1936, Mr. Democrat himself, Al Smith, the great American, came before the American people and charged that the leadership of his Party was taking the Party of Jefferson, Jackson, and Cleveland down the road under the banners of Marx, Lenin, and Stalin. And he walked away from his Party, and he never returned til the day he died—because to this day, the leadership of that Party has been taking that Party, that honorable Party, down the road in the image of the labor Socialist Party of England.

Now it doesn't require expropriation or confiscation of private property or business to impose socialism on a people. What does it mean whether you hold the deed to the—or the title to your business or property if the government holds the power of life and death over that business or property? And such machinery already exists. The government can find some charge to bring against any concern it chooses to prosecute. Every businessman has his own tale of harassment. Somewhere a perversion has taken place. Our natural, unalienable rights are now considered to be a dispensation of government, and freedom has never been so fragile, so close to slipping from our grasp as it is at this moment.

Our Democratic opponents seem unwilling to debate these issues. They want to make you and I believe that this is a contest between two men — that we're to choose just between two personalities.

Well what of this man that they would destroy — and in destroying, they would destroy that which he represents, the ideas that you and I hold dear? Is he the brash and shallow and trigger-happy man they say he is? Well I've been privileged to know him "when." I knew him long before he ever dreamed of trying for high office, and I can tell you personally I've never known a man in my life I believed so incapable of doing a dishonest or dishonorable thing.

This is a man who, in his own business before he entered politics, instituted a profit-sharing plan before unions had ever thought of it. He put in health and medical insurance for all his employees. He took 50 percent of the profits before taxes and set up a retirement program, a pension plan for all his employees. He sent monthly checks for life to an employee who was ill and couldn't work. He provides nursing care for the children of mothers who work in the stores. When Mexico was ravaged by the floods in the Rio Grande, he climbed in his airplane and flew medicine and supplies down there.

An ex-GI told me how he met him. It was the week before Christmas during the Korean War, and he was at the Los Angeles airport trying to get a ride home to Arizona for Christmas. And he said that [there were] a lot of servicemen there and no seats available on the planes. And then a voice came over the loudspeaker and said, "Any men in uniform wanting a ride to Arizona, go to runway such-and-such," and they went down there, and there was a fellow named Barry Goldwater sitting in his plane. Every day in those weeks before Christmas, all day long, he'd load up the plane, fly it to Arizona, fly them to their homes, fly back over to get another load.

During the hectic split-second timing of a campaign, this is a man who took time out to sit beside an old friend who was dying of cancer. His campaign managers were understandably impatient, but he said, "There aren't many left who care what happens to her. I'd like her to know I care." This is a man who said to his 19-year-old son, "There is no foundation like the rock of honesty and fairness, and when you begin to build your life on that rock, with the cement of the faith in God that you have, then you have a real start." This is not a man who could carelessly send other people's sons to war. And that is the issue of this campaign that makes all the other problems I've discussed academic, unless we realize we're in a war that must be won.

Those who would trade our freedom for the soup kitchen of the welfare state have told us they have a utopian solution of peace without victory. They call their policy "accommodation." And they say if we'll only avoid any direct confrontation with the enemy, he'll forget his evil ways and learn to love us. All who oppose them are indicted as warmongers. They say we offer simple answers to complex problems. Well, perhaps there is a simple answer—not an easy answer—but simple: If you and I have the courage to tell our elected officials that we want our national policy based on what we know in our hearts is morally right.

We cannot buy our security, our freedom from the threat of the bomb by committing an immorality so great as saying to a billion human beings now enslaved behind the Iron Curtain, "Give up your dreams of freedom because to save our own skins, we're willing to make a deal with your slave masters." Alexander Hamilton said, "A nation which can prefer disgrace to danger is prepared for a master, and deserves one." Now let's set the record straight. There's no argument over the choice between peace and war, but there's only one guaranteed way you can have peace—and you can have it in the next second—surrender.

Admittedly, there's a risk in any course we follow other than this, but every lesson of history tells us that the greater risk lies in appeasement, and this is the specter our well-meaning liberal friends refuse to face—that their policy of accommodation is appeasement, and it gives no choice between peace and war, only between fight or surrender. If we continue to accommodate, continue to back and retreat, eventually we have to face the final demand—the ultimatum. And what then—when Nikita Khrushchev has told his people he knows what our answer will be? He has told them that we're retreating under the pressure of the Cold War, and someday when the time comes to deliver the final ultimatum, our surrender will be voluntary, because by that time we will have been weakened from within spiritually, morally, and economically. He believes this because from our side he's heard voices pleading for "peace at any price" or "better Red than dead," or as one commentator put it, he'd rather "live on his knees than die on his feet." And therein lies the road to war, because those voices don't speak for the rest of us.

You and I know and do not believe that life is so dear and peace so sweet as to be purchased at the price of chains and slavery. If nothing in life is worth dying for, when did this begin—just in the face of this enemy? Or should Moses have told the children of Israel to live in slavery under the pharaohs? Should Christ have refused the cross? Should the patriots at Concord Bridge have thrown down their guns and refused to fire the shot heard 'round the world? The martyrs of history were not fools, and our honored dead who gave their lives to stop the advance of the Nazis didn't die in vain. Where, then, is the road to peace? Well it's a simple answer after all.

You and I have the courage to say to our enemies, "There is a price we will not pay." "There is a point beyond which they must not advance." And this—this is the meaning in the phrase of Barry Goldwater's "peace through strength." Winston Churchill said, "The destiny of man is not measured by material computations. When great forces are on the move in the world, we learn we're spirits—not animals." And he said, "There's something going on in time and space, and beyond time and space, which, whether we like it or not, spells duty."

You and I have a rendezvous with destiny.

We'll preserve for our children this, the last best hope of man on earth, or we'll sentence them to take the last step into a thousand years of darkness.

We will keep in mind and remember that Barry Goldwater has faith in us. He has faith that you and I have the ability and the dignity and the right to make our own decisions and determine our own destiny.

Thank you very much.

[Text of A Time for Choosing speech by Ronald Reagan courtesy The Miller Center, University of Virginia.]

# FOREWORD TO BONHOEFFER

**BY TIM KELLER**

I AM DELIGHTED THAT my friend Eric Metaxas has penned this volume on Dietrich Bonhoeffer. The English-speaking public needs to know far more than it does about his thought as well as his life. When I became a Christian in college, Bonhoeffer's Cost of Discipleship was one of the first books I read, followed not long after by his Life Together. Though his second book is perhaps the finest single volume I have ever read on the character of Christian community, it was the first book that set me on a lifelong journey to understand the meaning of grace.

It is impossible to understand Bonhoeffer's Nachfolge without becoming acquainted with the shocking capitulation of the German church to Hitler in the 1930's. How could the "church of Luther," that great teacher of the gospel, have ever come to such a place? The answer is that the true gospel, summed up by Bonhoeffer as costly grace, had been lost. On the one hand, the church had become marked by formalism. That meant going to church and hearing that God just loves and forgives everyone, so it doesn't really matter much how you live. Bonhoeffer called this cheap grace. On the other hand, there was legalism, or salvation by law and good works. Legalism meant that God loves you because you have pulled yourself together and are trying to live a good, disciplined life.

Both these impulses made it possible for Hitler to come to power. . . As one, Germany lost hold of the brilliant balance of the gospel that Luther so persistently expounded—"We are saved by faith alone, but not by faith which is alone." That is, we are saved, not by anything we do, but by grace. Yet if we have truly understood and believed the gospel, it will change what we do and how we live.

By the time of Hitler's ascension, much of the German church understood grace only as an abstract acceptance—"God forgives, that's his job." But we know that true grace comes to us by costly sacrifice. And if God was willing to go to the cross and endure such pain and absorb such a cost in order to save us, then we must live sacrificially as we serve others. Anyone who truly understands how God's grace comes to us will have a changed life. That's the gospel, not salvation by law, or by cheap grace, but by costly grace. Costly grace changes you from the inside out. Neither law or cheap grace can do that.

This lapse couldn't happen to us, today, surely, could it? Certainly it could. We still have a lot of legalism and moralism in our churches. In reaction to that, many churches want to talk only about God's love and acceptance. They don't like talking about Jesus' death on the cross to satisfy divine wrath and justice. Some even call it "divine child abuse." Yet if they are not careful, they run the risk of falling into the belief in "cheap grace"—a non costly love from a non-holy God who just loves and accepts us as we are. That will never change anyone's life.

So it looks like we still need to listen to Bonhoeffer and others who go deep in discussing the nature of the gospel.

-------------------------

*Timothy Keller is an American pastor, theologian and Christian apologist. He is best known as the founding pastor of Redeemer Presbyterian Church in New York, and the author of The New York Times bestselling books The Reason for God: Belief in an Age of Skepticism.*

# THE UNITED 'STATISTS' OF AMERICA?

## April 20, 2015

### BY DR. PETER A. LILLBACK

"A GOVERNMENT THAT IS BIG enough to give you whatever you want is big enough to take away everything you have." This political aphorism is often wrongly attributed to Thomas Jefferson. Although said by Gerald Ford, nevertheless, Jefferson would likely have agreed since he observed, "The natural progress of things is for liberty to yield, and government to gain ground."[1]

Statism extols this seemingly inexorable tendency to centralize power in the state. Rather than lodging power in individuals and independent bodies of government, statists believe that the highest good of life is human government.[2] A corollary of statism is that government is best able to meet the needs of its people. Statists are committed to an ever increasing role of government in all spheres of life. In statist philosophy, family, church, business, religion, education and local government should all be under the control of a vast centralized governmental bureaucracy. If followed to its logical conclusion, statism leads to some form of totalitarianism. Ultimately, the emphasis on the collective destroys the significance of the individual.

A prime example of collective statecraft swallowing up individual liberty is communist ideology. Communism is a statist movement motivated by socialistic doctrine. The classic source for this is Karl Marx's *The Communist Manifesto*.[3] At the request of the Communist League, Marx wrote the *Manifesto* which was first published in Brussels in February 1848. Marx declared:

> It is high time that Communists should openly, in the efface of the whole world, publish their views, their aims, and their tendencies, and meet this nursery tale of the spectre of Communism with a Manifesto of the party itself.[4]

Communism's statist vision is to be achieved through the class struggle between the Bourgeois (industrialists/capitalist) and Proletarians (modern working class or laborers). Marx explains, "The history of all hitherto existing society is the history of class struggles....In short, the Communists everywhere support every revolutionary movement against the existing social and political order of things.... They openly declare that their ends can be attained only by the forcible overthrow of all existing social conditions."[5]

Marx summarized communism's tenets with remarkable and radical goals:

> The immediate aim of the Communists is...overthrow of the bourgeois supremacy, conquest of political power by the proletariat....
> In this sense, the theory of the Communists may be summed up on the single sentence: Abolition of private property....Abolition of the Family! Even the most radical flare up at this infamous proposal of the Communists. On what foundation is the present family, the bourgeois family, based? On capital. But, you will say, we destroy the most hallowed of relations, when we replace home education by social....But you communists would introduce community of women. The Communists are further reproached with desiring to abolish countries and nationality....The charges against Communism made from a religious, a philosophical, and generally, from an ideological standpoint, are not deserving of serious examination.[6]

Yet even with such unbiblical commitments, various schools of Christianity have embraced elements of communist teaching under the rubrics of "Christian Communism", "Liberation Theology" or "Christian Socialism". Marx anticipated this and ironically remarked in the *Manifesto*:

> Nothing is easier than to give Christian asceticism a socialist tinge. Has not Christianity declaimed against private property, against marriage, against the state? Has it not preached in the place of these, charity and poverty, celibacy and mortification of the flesh, monastic life and Mother Church? Christian socialism is but the holy water with which the priest consecrates the heart-burnings of the aristocrat.[7]

While Marx recognized that socialism is a milder form of communism, clearly not every socialist or every statist ideology holds to the more radical tenets of communism. Yet, when the often heard concept of "social justice" is employed, it implies an enforced redistribution of wealth. This raises the legitimate query whether social justice legitimizes injustice by the diminishing or violating the rights of others by despoiling them of their personal property. Economically or politically speaking, it is not possible to have complete liberty and complete equality at the same time. Statism recognizes this tension and solves it by making the government the ultimate arbiter of liberty and equality, administering them as it alone deems best. In a statist regime, the state alone is free.

The statist vision has advanced with alacrity in the United States. The regulatory state in America increasingly extends the reach of federal power. The proliferation of executive orders and legislation from the bench manifest a metastasis of government power beyond constitutional limits. Federal taxation escalates even though it is a truism that the power to tax is the power to destroy. We should not forget what James Madison wrote in the *National Gazette*, January 19, 1792, "Every word of [the *Constitution*] decides a question between power and liberty."[8]

Understandably, there is a growing concern among many Americans. Could we be losing our Constitution? These fears are fueled by courts that seem to change the Constitution at will. And legislators and executives seem to bend the Constitution to achieve their political aims. Is this just a bit of political hysteria generated by uncertain times?

# I. GEORGE WASHINGTON'S PROPHETIC CONCERN ABOUT THE CONSTITUTION

But make no mistake about it, the loss of the American Constitution is not a recent concern. It was a matter that troubled the newly elected President George Washington. In April 1789 George Washington prepared an address for Congress. It touched on a host of important matters that would impact the new Congress that was soon to meet for the first time under the newly adopted US Constitution. One of his most extraordinary insights in this lengthy document was his concern for the long term survival of the new Constitution.

To understand Washington's concerns, we must carefully read his classic language. To help, I will outline his points and state them in simpler words in italics. Then, I will quote his actual words. Please consider these seven points that our Founding Father made about the long term survivability of our Constitution.

1. *Washington was not a prophet and could not make a final prediction about the ultimate fate of the Constitution.* "I pretend to no unusual foresight into futurity, and therefore cannot undertake to decide, with certainty, what may be its ultimate fate."
2. *In our uncertain world good things have often ended up as disappointing evils and this could happen with our Constitution too.* "If a promised good should terminate in an unexpected evil, it would not be a solitary example of disappointment in this mutable state of existence."
3. *If we lose our Constitution's blessings of liberty, it would not be the first time that human foolishness has squandered the blessings of heaven.* "If the blessings of Heaven showered thick around us should be spilled on the ground or converted to curses, through the fault of those for whom they were intended, it would not be the first instance of folly or perverseness in short-sighted mortals."
4. *The word of God's revelation of the Christian religion provides an eternal example of the fact that the best human organizations can be used for evil ends.* "The blessed Religion revealed in the word of God will remain an eternal and awful monument to prove that the best Institutions may be abused by human depravity; and that they

may even, in some instances be made subservient to the vilest of purposes." (Washington is here referring to the events surrounding the crucifixion of Jesus Christ.)

5. *America's future power-hungry leaders could get away with a disregard of the Constitution's limitations and harm our unalienable rights because the voters have become lazy or selfish.* "Should, hereafter, those who are entrusted with the management of this government, incited by the lust of power and prompted by the Supineness or venality of their Constituents, overleap the known barriers of this Constitution and violate the unalienable rights of humanity:"

6. *No mere human document is eternal and indestructible even if it began with God's favor and was declared to be holy.* "it will only serve to show, that no compact among men (however provident in its construction and sacred in its ratification) can be pronounced everlasting and inviolable,"

7. *No words on a piece of paper can withstand unbridled political ambition that remains unchecked due to an immoral electorate.* "and if I may so express myself, that no Wall of words, that no mound of parchment can be so formed as to stand against the sweeping torrent of boundless ambition on the one side, aided by the sapping current of corrupted morals on the other."[9]

This almost sounds like the evening news. Was Washington prophesying the destruction of our country that we might be seeing in our own day?

## II. RELIGIOUS LIBERTY AS A CHECK ON GOVERNMENTAL TYRANNY

Where then does government power come from? In his Inaugural Address on January 20, 1961, John F. Kennedy answered this question when he affirmed, "...the rights of man come not from the generosity of the state but from the hand of God." In a recent editorial, Cal Thomas shows, however, that this is not the view of everyone today:

It isn't often that a member of the media reveals the philosophy behind his political ideology, but last week, CNN anchor Chris Cuomo outed himself. In an exchange with Alabama Chief Justice

Roy Moore about Moore's refusal to adhere to a federal appellate judge's order to ignore the state constitution and begin granting marriage licenses to same-sex couples, Moore said "...our rights contained in the Bill of Rights do not come from the Constitution, they come from God."

Cuomo disagreed: "Our laws do not come from God, your honor, and you know that. They come from man."

Obviously, Cuomo flunked civics. Does he really believe that man is responsible for bestowing rights, and can therefore take those rights away as he sees fit? That a right bestowed today by a governing body of mere mortals can be invalidated by another body, say, following an election? That my rights and yours are as fluid as quicksilver and dependent on who sits in the big chair in Washington?

It is not a new debate, but a debate worth renewing.[10]

The rising tide of American statism is evident when issues of religion in the public square are raised. Should the government be able to prohibit Christian military chaplains from praying in Jesus' name? Is the government acting constitutionally when it mandates abortion services by federal law as with the Affordable Care Act, or when courts declare the supremacy of sexual liberty over religious liberty in conflicts arising from the normalization of homosexuality? Thomas Jefferson's first impressions of the new American Constitution seem right. After reviewing the new constitution in France, he worried about the potential for a judicial oligarchy. This was due to what seemed to him to be the constitution's insufficient checks on the judiciary.

Religious liberty is a safeguard against governments' attempts to increase their powers. The lack of religious liberty tends to nurture a tyranny that suppresses the individual liberties of citizens. Thus religious liberty has foundational significance for western civilization that has asserted that authentic personal liberty is impossible without religious liberty. Such was the thrust of President Franklin D. Roosevelt's "Four Freedoms" address given to the US Congress on January 6, 1941:

In the future days which we seek to make secure, we look forward to a world founded upon four essential human freedoms.

The first is freedom of speech and expression—everywhere in the world. The second is freedom of every person to worship God in his own way—everywhere in the world. The third is freedom from want—which, translated into world terms, means economic undertakings which will secure to every nation a healthy peacetime life for its inhabitants—everywhere in the world. The fourth is freedom from fear—which, translated into world terms, means a worldwide reduction of armaments to such a point and in such a thorough fashion that no nation will be in a position to commit an act of physical aggression against any neighbor—anywhere in the world. . . . Freedom means the supremacy of human rights everywhere.

Religious liberty became broadly recognized as it is a commitment of the United Nations. *The Universal Declaration of Human Rights*, adopted by the United Nations on December 10, 1948 proclaims:

Everyone has the right to freedom of thought, conscience and religion; this right includes freedom to change his religion or belief, and freedom, either alone or in community with others and in public or private, to manifest his religion or belief in teaching, practice, worship and observance.

Religious liberty is a tenet of today's Roman Catholic faith. Pope John Paul II said in his Message for the World Day of Peace, January 1, 1988, "Every violation of religious freedom, whether open or hidden, does fundamental damage to the cause of peace, like violations of other fundamental rights of the human person."

And it has hitherto been an indisputable premise of American values. President George W. Bush declared on May 7, 2001,

It is not an accident that freedom of religion is one of the central freedoms in our Bill of Rights. It is the first freedom of the human soul: the right to speak the words that God places in our mouths. We must stand for that freedom in our country. We must speak for that freedom in the world.

The erosion of religious liberty in America should be a concern for everyone.

Ultimately, statist views claim the ground previously reserved for God as the transcendent source of true liberty and ultimate justice. And as statism tends to be secular and atheistic in nature, we should remember that atheism inherently hates religion in general and theism in particular.[11] Atheism holds religion in all its forms to be intellectual delusions or tools of oppression. Thus as Christianity's influence in American culture diminishes, atheistic ideologies and their statist commitments increase their assaults upon religious liberty. If we are not "one nation under God", then we are but a nation under government. The United States then becomes United Statism.

## III. THE FOUNDERS' VIEW OF GOVERNMENT IN DEPENDENCE UPON GOD

So what did the American founders believe about God and government? For statists, the state is for all practical purposes divine in character. But was this the vision of America's founders? Does "the separation of church and state" mean the separation of God and government? Did the framers of America's government hope their unique political creation would become divine? To answer, we now address the American Founders' vision of the relationship of God and government.

While the early American leaders did not use the term "statism", they recognized the danger that an all-powerful government presented to liberty. Indeed, they absolutely opposed absolute government. Their perspective emerged from their notions of God, government, monarchy, tyranny and despotism. So when they set out to set up their state, they designed it to be diametrically opposed to the statist perspective.

Just how big was the fledgling government of the United States to become? A review of the early statements of the American patriots show their political philosophy was shaped by theism rather than statism. If statism desires a divine state, theism sees that state is inferior to the transcendent being and justice of God. For example, in March 1776, the Continental Congress agreed to the following resolution for appointing a fast:

> In times of impending calamity and distress; when the liberties of America are imminently endangered by the secret machinations and open assaults of an insidious and vindictive administration, it becomes the indispensable duty of these hitherto free and happy colonies, with true penitence of heart, and the most reverent devotion, publickly to acknowledge the over ruling providence of God; to confess and deplore our offences against him; and to supplicate his interposition for averting the threatened danger, and prospering our strenuous efforts in the cause of freedom, virtue, and posterity.

Clearly, the Continental Congress did not desire an all-powerful state. This was precisely what they were fleeing from in the form of a tyrannical monarchy. Against despotic power, they appealed to divine power above the earthly state. God's rescuing grace in the face of a powerful malevolent state pervades the Founders' call for prayer, fasting and humiliation.

> The Congress, therefore, considering the warlike preparations of the British Ministry to subvert our invaluable rights and priviledges, and to reduce us by fire and sword, by the savages of the wilderness, and our own domestics, to the most abject and ignominious bondage: Desirous, at the same time, to have people of all ranks and degrees duly impressed with a solemn sense of God's superintending providence, and of their duty, devoutly to rely, in all their lawful enterprizes, on his aid and direction, Do earnestly recommend, that Friday, the Seventeenth day of May next, be observed by the said colonies as a day of humiliation, fasting, and prayer; that we may, with united hearts, confess and bewail our manifold sins and transgressions, and, by a sincere repentance and amendment of life, appease his righteous displeasure, and through the merits and mediation of *Jesus Christ*, obtain his pardon and forgiveness; humbly

imploring his assistance to frustrate the cruel purposes of our un-
natural enemies; and by inclining their hearts to justice and benevolence, prevent the further effusion of kindred blood.

But if, continuing deaf to the voice of reason and humanity, and in-
flexibly bent on desolation and war, they constrain us to repel their
hostile invasions by open resistance, that it may please the Lord of
Hosts, the God of Armies, to animate our officers and soldiers with
invincible fortitude, to guard and protect them in the day of battle,
and to crown the continental arms, by sea and land, with victory
and success: Earnestly beseeching him to bless our civil rulers, and
the representatives of the people, in their several assemblies and
conventions; to preserve and strengthen their union to inspire them
with an ardent, disinterested love of their country; to give wisdom
and stability to their counsels; and direct them to the most effica-
cious measures for establishing the rights of America on the most
honourable and permanent basis--That he would be graciously
pleased to bless all his people in these colonies with health and
plenty, and grant that a spirit of incorruptible patriotism, and of
pure undefiled religion, may universally prevail; and this continent be speedily restored to the blessings of peace and liberty, and
enabled to transmit them inviolate the latest posterity. And it is
recommended to Christians of all denominations, to assemble for
public worship, and abstain from servile labour on the said day.[12]

Rather than a divine-like state, they advocated a government that reflected
the Christian perspective that men "ought to obey God rather than man"
(Acts 5:29) as is reflected in their Thanksgiving Proclamation dated November 1, 1777. Their battle was done in obedience to God and in light of the
gospel of Jesus Christ:

Forasmuch as it is the indispensable duty of all men to adore the
superintending providence of Almighty God; to acknowledge with
gratitude their obligation to him for benefits received, and to im-
plore such farther blessings as they stand in need of; and it having
pleased him in his abundant mercy not only to continue to us the

innumerable bounties of his common providence, but also to smile upon us in the prosecution of a just and necessary war, for the defence and establishment of our unalienable rights and liberties; particularly in that he hath been pleased in so great a measure to prosper the means used for the support of our troops and to crown our arms with most signal success: It is therefore recommended to the legislative or executive powers of these United States, to set apart Thursday, the eighteenth day of December next, for solemn thanksgiving and praise; that with one heart and one voice the good people may express the grateful feelings of their hearts, and consecrate themselves to the service of their divine benefactor; and that together with their sincere acknowledgments and offerings, they may join the penitent confession of their manifold sins, whereby they had forfeited every favour, and their humble and earnest supplication that it may please God, through the merits of Jesus Christ, mercifully to forgive and blot them out of remembrance; that it may please him graciously to afford his blessing on the governments of these states respectively, and prosper the public council of the whole; to inspire our commanders both by land and by sea, and all under them, with that wisdom and fortitude which may render them fit instruments, under the providence of Almighty God, to secure for these United States the greatest of all human blessings, independence and peace; that it may please him to prosper the trade and manufactures of the people and the labour of the husbandman, that our land may yet yield its increase; to take schools and seminaries of education, so necessary for cultivating the principles of true liberty, virtue and piety, under his nurturing hand, and to prosper the means of religion for the promotion and enlargement of that kingdom which consisteth "in righteousness, peace and joy in the Holy Ghost. And it is further recommended, that servile labour, and such recreation as, though at other times innocent, may be unbecoming the purpose of this appointment, be omitted on so solemn an occasion."[13]

These historic congressional statements illustrate their belief in the transcendence of God over government as well as the Founders' negative experience with an all-powerful government.

## IV. SOURCES FOR THE FOUNDERS' VIEW OF GOD OVER GOVERNMENT AS GUARANTEE OF LIBERTY

The notions of resistance to the absolutism of government came to the American framers of government through their knowledge of the long history of western civilization. They were conversant with the legacy of powerful government entities as implied in terms such as Constantinianism and Caesaropapism. They knew the medieval struggle with tyrannical popes that gave rise to the conciliarist movement that sought to rescue the church from papal absolutism. The English struggle with the abuse of royal power had produced the Magna Charta, the English Bill of Rights and the emergence of parliamentary authority, each of which were part of the arsenal of their political reflection.

### 1. The Reformer, John Calvin

The Protestant Reformers, Calvin in particular, had a demonstrable impact on the thinking of several of the early American political thinkers with regard to the republican theory of government. When Calvin had settled in Geneva, he produced his 1543 edition of the *Institutes*. Therein he introduced into his theology an explicit statement of political preference:

> For if the three forms of government which the philosophers discuss be considered in themselves, I will not deny that aristocracy, or a system compounded of aristocracy and democracy (*vel aristocratian vel temperatum ex ipsa et politia statum*) far excels all others.[14]

The politics of republican government were a hallmark of Calvin's thought as McNeill summarizes,

> It need not surprise us to find that from his Commentary on Seneca's Treatise on Clemency of 1532 until that hour in 1564 when from his deathbed he urged the magistrates of Geneva so to rule as to 'preserve this republic in its present happy condition,' his writings are strewn with penetrating comments on the policies of rulers and illuminating passages on the principles of government.[15]

An eminent Catholic historian, E. Jarry, states that 'in the political domain, Calvinist ideas are at the origin of the revolution which from the 18th to the 19th centuries gave birth and growth to the parliamentary democracies of Anglo-Saxon type."[16] Philip Schaff, church historian, wrote: "The principles of the Republic of the United States can be traced through the intervening link of Puritanism to Calvinism, which, with all its theological rigor, has been the chief educator of manly characters and promoter of constitutional freedom in modern times."

## 2. French Huguenots and the Monarchomachs

Moreover, the American Founders personally knew, knew of, or had even descended from persecuted French Huguenots. These Calvinistic Protestants had developed extensive theories of resistance to tyranny developed in their struggle with the Inquisition and an absolutist divine-right monarchy. The French political theorists of the time have been dubbed, the monarchomachs, meaning "enemies of the monarch" or "fighters against the king." They united on the conception that magistrates were created for the people and not people for their rulers. Three great monarchomach classics were produced. The first appeared in 1573 written by Francois Hotman, entitled, *Franco-Gallia*. The following year in 1574, Theodore Beza's *Du droit des magistrats sur leurs sujets* was published. Finally in 1579 the *Vindicae contra Tyrannos* was released written by Philippe Duplessis-Mornay.[17]

The Huguenot monarchomachs developed various theories that legitimated the resistance of a tyrannical prince by his subjects.[18] As these are considered, one can hear a clear echo of them in the American context as well. The leading examples are:

### (1) The Constitutional Argument[19]
The writers sought to operate within the expressed terms and structure of the constitution that they were governed by.

### (2) Theory of Sovereignty: The People Create the King[20]
Political sovereignty emerges from the people. Even in hereditary monarchies, magistrates are created by the people. The *Vindiciae* declares, "never was a man born with a crown on his head and the scepter in his hand."

### (3) Appeal to Inferior Magistrates[21]

Resistance was not the fruit of anarchy but of ordered governmental structure. The inferior magistrates had as part of their duty the correction of the king. "Only the subordinate magistrates could act in the name of the people and even appeal to foreign powers for help against a tyrant."[22]

### (4) Dual Covenant Idea.

"The covenant principle of limited monarchy was further advanced by the *Vindiciae contra tyrannos* (1579), written in part by Philip du Plessis Mornay. More explicitly than in earlier treatises the sacred covenant of ruler and people here involves a covenant of both with God."[23]

The delegation of the people's power to the monarch by their consent is conditional because it is a covenant or contract. "Inferior magistrates" if necessary could lead resistance. This is because all government involves two covenants, one between God and the general population inclusive of both the king and his subjects, and a second between the monarch and his subjects. A king who broke these contracts, lost God's support and the legitimate expectation of human obedience.[24]

### (5) Corporate Resistance View

The king is a lesser universe than the people, but a greater individual than any person, thus resistance must be the work of the people, not of an individual seditious person.[25] In this view, resistance was not anarchical because it did not legitimate individual subjects' resistance to the king, or permit assassination or tyrannicide. This follows from popular consent, which brings a government into existence. The formation of a government is accomplished by the people considered collectively. Mornay argues that the ruler is a *minor universis* (a lesser universe) when compared to all the people who create the monarchy, but the king is a *maior singulis* (a greater individual) as every other individual inclusive of magistrates are lesser than the king as individuals. So no private citizen on his own can ever have the right to resist a legitimately enthroned monarch. Thus, "the people 'create the prince not as individuals but all together'" and "their rights against him are the rights of a corporation, not the rights" of a single member. Accordingly, "private individuals who 'draw the sword' against their kings are thus 'seditious, no matter how just the cause may be.'"[26]

## (6) Universal Human Dignity

In the aftermath of the St. Bartholomew's Day Massacre,[27] a lesser known work, the *Reveille-matin*, asked that "all our Catholics, our patriots, our good neighbours and all the rest of the French, who are treated worse than beasts, should wake up this time so as to perceive their misery and take counsel together how to remedy their misfortunes."[28] This was a cry for all to see necessary limits on the king's authority. By the king's denial of the humanity of his subjects, he himself was no longer a public person. Thus he was no longer worthy of respect and protection from revolt, but a tyrant who usurped the attributes of God, who alone can take life.

## (7) Separation of Powers

Paul Fuhrmann offers a concise summary of Mornay and Monarchomachists' views on the separation of powers:

> "Mornay caught sight of the fact that if the legislative power is the same as the executive, there are then no bounds to the executive power. The only safeguard of the liberty and security of persons is to be found in the separation of political powers. With imposing gravity, Mornay and the Monarchomachists set forth the four great principles: sovereignty of the nation, political contract, representative government, and the separation of powers that really makes up all our modern constitutions."[29]

Thus, this assessment underlines the often overlooked contribution of Huguenot thinkers to the development of modern political theories.

### 3. The English Civil War: Scottish Covenanter and English Puritan Resistance to the King

Another important force on the American Founders in terms of resistance to absolute government become tyrannical is found in the context of the English Civil War. The Covenanters[30] have long been identified with the Presbyterian resistance to the British Crown in Scotland.[31] The King was not a king in the Scottish Kirk, but a member:

> Presbyterian partisans adopted the two kingdom theory of church-state relations, …Although this doctrine also taught the Christian magistrate's freedom from clerical dictation, its practical effect in Scotland was to promote the exclusion of the king as king from ecclesiastical decision. "there is two Kings and twa Kingdomes in Scotland" went Melville's famous rebuke. "Thair is Chryst Jesus the King, and his kingdome the Kirk, whase subject King James the Saxt is, and of whase kingdome nocht a king, nor a lord, nor a heid, bot a member!"[32]

The English context also produced Puritan Independency[33] and the Westminster Standards[34] in the context of a civil war against the British King who was the head of the Anglican Church. Charles I had continued his father James I's religious persecution of the Puritans in England and the Presbyterians in Scotland. But Charles met such strong opposition in Knox's Scotland that he had to call for the election of a Parliament to raise men and resources to carry on the war. In 1637, the Scottish National Covenant was signed, that abolished the Anglican Episcopal form of church government. This was prompted by the unsuccessful attempt to impose by force Anglican worship on the Scottish Calvinists.

But to the King's surprise and anger, the people elected a Parliament with a majority of Puritans, which the King then dissolved, calling for another election. The second Parliament, however, had an even greater number of Puritans. But when Charles ordered it to dissolve, Parliament refused, forcing Charles to field an army to force the Parliament to obey him. Soon Parliament called upon the Scottish Presbyterians to join them. Their army was led by Oliver Cromwell defeated Charles, who was beheaded 1649. The Commonwealth was established and Oliver Cromwell became the Lord Protector of England and Scotland. Cromwell ruled from 1648 until 1660. But with Cromwell's death, there was no one of his stature to lead the Parliament and Charles II ascended to his father's throne.

During the more than five years of civil war, the Westminster Assembly sought to reform the Church of England. The delegates to the Assembly included one hundred twenty-one ministers, all except for two had been ordained by a bishop in the Church of England. They began their work at the Westminster Abbey in London, on July 1, 1643. After giving up the attempt to rework the Anglican Church's Thirty-Nine Articles of Religion, they began the production of a new Confession of Faith. The *Westminster Confession of Faith* was finished by year's end in 1646, and approved by Parliament in 1648.

All of this is relevant to the founding of what Washington called "the American experiment in republican government" since many of his soldiers and officers were of English Puritan and Scottish Presbyterian descent and carried with them deep commitments to resist tyranny as an act of faithful obedience to the higher law of God that was to govern human political entities.

## 4. Reformation Resistance in the Netherlands and Other European Countries

Similar efforts at religiously based resistance in the Reformation era can be found across Europe in Anglicanism,[35] the Palatinate and German Reformed churches[36] and in Eastern Europe in Hungary and Poland.[37] Dutch Calvinism[38] also had a long struggle with Spanish domination and Roman Catholic persecution. The political legacy of Calvin can be heard in William of Orange's famous Apology in 1581 during the revolt of the Netherlands from Spanish rule. McNeill states,

> His position was that obedience to Philip II was strictly conditional on fulfillment of the king's obligation contracted under oath and that the rebelling nobles of the Netherlands, standing in the place of the ephors of Sparta, have a duty to support a good king and restrain an unfaithful one. In the Netherlands, as in Scotland, the Reformation involved an armed revolution, but the struggle was of longer duration and greater intensity.[39]

## V. FOUR CLASSIC STUDIES OF LAW AND GOVERNMENT THAT SHAPED EARLY AMERICAN THOUGHT

Several post-reformation writers wrote substantial treatises on political themes that grew out of the themes developed and honed in the fires of Reformation controversies. These works in turn laid the foundation for modern Western political thought and left a legacy that helped to shape the Protestant colonies in the New World. From this intellectual basis, a concept of a law above the state developed that enabled the American Revolution to occur on what was viewed a just basis. But for this to occur, it was anything but a statist conception.

### A. Samuel Rutherford's Lex Rex.[40]

The main theme of *Lex rex* is that all rightful authority lies in law, whether it is authority of king, estates, populace, or kirk. The king is truly king only when he identifies himself with the law, and only to the degree that he succeeds in voicing and implementing law. "*Rex est lex viva, animata, loquens lex*: The king is a living, breathing, and speaking Law." His function is necessary because men naturally avoid voluntary submission to law, "so is the King the Law reduced in practice." The nearer the king personifies the law, the more king he is; "in his remotest distance from Law and Reason, he is a Tyrant.[41]

Rutherford sees the origin of government in God and in the people's act of initiating particular political systems, all forms of which are lawful and originally, including monarchy, were elective. He followed Mornay's *Vindiciae* in seeing three parties to the covenant—God, the ruler, and the people—and two compacts, one between God and the total community, and the other between the ruler and the people.[42] Rutherford writes, "The Lord and the people give the crown by one and the same action;…seeing the people maketh him a King covenant-wise, and conditionally, so he rule according to God's Law and the people resigning their power to him for their safety…; it is certain God giveth a King that same way, by that same very act of the people."[43]

> If the king breaks the covenant with God, the political covenant
> is shattered and the ruler was no longer a lawful king. In such a
> case the people "are presumed to have no King…and…to have the

power in themselves as if they had not appointed any King at all."
(*Lex rex*, pp. 96ff.)

Rutherford recognizes legitimate popular resistance, for by the injustice of magistrates, he asserts that they abandon their lawful office and forfeit all claim on the obedience of religious men. The allegation that people would revolt for a few infractions of the covenant, Rutherford rejects saying that Tyranny will be obvious and the people may judge. "The people have a naturall throne of policie in their conscience to give warning, and materially sentence against the King as a Tyrant....Where Tyranny is more obscure, ... the King keepeth possession; but I deny that Tyranny can be obscure long."

Both the people and the King are bound in covenant: the people are bound in the covenant no less than the king, and the king's duty is to compel them to observe its terms. "Each may compel the other to mutual performance."

### B. John Althusius[44]

In the Protestant Netherlands, John Althusius, a Geneva-trained German, wrote *Politics Methodically Set Forth (Politica methodice digesta*, 1603). This treatise advocates a plan of government in which provision is made for maximum cooperation between rulers and people.[45]

Althusius published what Thomas O. Hueglin calls "the first full-bodied political theory of the modern age."[46] Althusius begins, "Politics is the art of consociating men for the purpose of establishing, cultivating, and conserving social life among them. Whence it is called 'symbiotics.' The subject matter of politics is therefore consociation, in which the symbiotes pledge themselves each to the other , by an explicit or tacit pact, to mutual communication of whatever is useful and necessary for the harmonious exercise of social life."[47]

Thus, the fundamental or constitutional law of the commonwealth is, in the words of Althusius: "Nothing other than certain pacts by which many cities and provinces come together and agree to establish and defend one and the same commonwealth by common work, counsel and aid." Neither is there any doubt about the historical example to which he referred regularly. In the preface to the second edition, he wrote: I more frequently use examples from sacred scripture because it has God or pious men as its author, and because I consider that no polity from the beginning of the world has been more wisely and perfectly constructed than the polity of the Jews. We err, I believe, whenever in similar circumstances we depart from it.[48]

It is clear that Althusius carried forward the Reformers' concern that the law of the state be grounded in the law of God:

> The rule of living, obeying, and administering, is the will of God alone, which is the way of life, and the law of things to be done and to be omitted. It is necessary that the magistrate rule, appoint, and examine all the business of his administration with this law as a touchstone and measure, unless he wishes to rule the ship of state as an unreliable vessel at sea, and to wander about and move at random. ....This rule, which is solely God's will for men manifested in his law, is called law in the general sense that it is a precept for doing those things that pertain to living a pious, holy, just, and suitable life. That is to say, it pertains to the duties that are to be performed toward God and one's neighbor, and to the love of God and one's neighbor[49]

### C. Hugo Grotius[50]

Hugo Grotius' *Right of War and Peace* (De jure belli et pacis, 1625) makes him the founder of modern international law. Central to his thought is the concept of a natural law identical with the law of God. It is so fixed that God himself could not change it. This law resides in human nature and is inseparable from it. When a ruler attempts some action in defiance of this law of nature he must be disobeyed and may be deposed and even punished with death.[51]

### D. John Locke

John Locke was highly influential in the thinking of the American Founders. His *Second Treatise of Government*, published in England in 1689 and printed in the American colonies in 1773, made a substantial impact on the Founders' political thought.[52] This is significant for our consideration of statism because Locke sees political sovereignty as lodged in the people and only secondarily in the hands of executives. Political leaders serve as rulers with only delegated not absolute power.

Locke reasoned that humans are equal in the state of nature. They possess natural rights that allow them to exist freely from any other rule than their own. However, societies develop for the common good. And then, people freely give up some of their natural freedom for the enjoyment of the benefits of social order. But since power and freedom were always theirs, should irremediable injustices occur, as with despotic leaders who misuse their delegated power, people have an indefeasible right to reclaim their original power. Thus the people retain the right to dissolve an unjust government when it is in their best interest. This view utterly rejects the statist claim that ultimate power is in the hands of the state.

Rutherford, Althusius, Grotius and Locke were towering political thinkers that shaped the anti-statist political thought of early colonial America.

## VI. THE DECLARATION OF INDEPENDENCE: THE AMERICAN COMMITMENT TO LIMITED GOVERNMENT

These culturally inherited understandings of the right to resist the excesses of tyrannical power by the early American Colonists blossomed in the context of the Stamp Act in 1765. The British parliament sought to find a way to refill the king's coffers after the draining expenses of the globally waged and successful war with France. In North America, this was called the French and Indian War. British efforts to enforce the collection of various taxes prompted the slogans of colonial resistance: "No taxation without representation" and "Taxation without representation is tyranny!" The word "tyranny" is found some 30 times in George Washington's writings.

A consideration of the Declaration of Independence reflects the rejection of absolute political power as well as the inherent right of the people to protect their God-given rights. The document begins, "IN CONGRESS, July 4, 1776. The unanimous Declaration of the thirteen united States of America". Some of its famous phrases reflect the ideas of the subordination of the state to the people, the right of resistance to tyranny and the subordination of the people to the higher law of God.

1. Statements that subordinate political power to the people:
   - When in the Course of human events, it becomes necessary for one **people to dissolve the political bands** which have connected them with another, and to assume among the powers of the earth, the separate and equal station to which the Laws of Nature and of Nature's God entitle them, a decent respect to the opinions of mankind requires that they should declare the causes which impel them to the separation.
   - That to secure these rights, **Governments** are instituted among Men, **deriving their just powers from the consent of the governed**,
   - That whenever any Form of Government becomes destructive of these ends, it is the **Right of the People to alter or to abolish it**, and to institute new Government, laying its foundation on such principles and organizing its powers in such form, as to them shall seem most likely to effect their Safety and Happiness.
   - But when a long train of abuses and usurpations, pursuing invariably the same Object evinces a design to reduce them under absolute Despotism, **it is their right, it is their duty, to throw off such Government**, and to provide new Guards for their future security.—
   - **We**, therefore, the Representatives of the united States of America, in General Congress, Assembled, appealing to the Supreme Judge of the world for the rectitude of our intentions, **do**, in the Name, and by Authority of the good People of these Colonies, solemnly publish and **declare**, That **these United Colonies are, and of Right ought to be Free and Independent States**; that they are Absolved from all Allegiance to the British Crown, and that **all political connection** between them and the State of Great Britain, **is and ought to be totally dissolved**;

2. Statements that reflect that their resistance is a response to tyranny:
   - That whenever any Form of Government becomes **destructive** of these ends
   - The history of the present King of Great Britain is a history of repeated injuries and usurpations, all having in direct object the establishment of an **absolute Tyranny** over these States.

- But when a long train of abuses and usurpations, pursuing invariably the same Object evinces a design to reduce them under **absolute Despotism**, it is their right, it is their duty, to throw off such Government, and to provide new Guards for their future security.—
- Our repeated Petitions have been answered only by repeated injury. A Prince whose character is thus marked by every act which may define a **Tyrant**, is unfit to be the ruler of a free people.

3.  Statements that recognize that their actions are taken under God:
    - … all men are created equal, that they are endowed by their **Creator** with certain unalienable Rights, that among these are Life, Liberty and the pursuit of Happiness.
    - …the Laws of Nature and of Nature's **God**
    - …appealing to the **Supreme Judge of the world** for the rectitude of our intentions
    - …for the support of this Declaration, with a firm reliance on the protection of **divine Providence**, we mutually pledge to each other our Lives, our Fortunes and our sacred Honor.

The Declaration of Independence is not only a statement of liberty it is Liberty's manifesto against statism!

## VII. WASHINGTON'S FAREWELL ADDRESS AND RELIGIOUS LIBERTY

The motivations for the US Constitution included greater powers for governmental efficiency than provided by the Articles of Confederation. Yet the Framers did not want to grant so much power to the new government that there would be a loss of liberty. Washington's Farewell Address provides a succinct statement of the Founders' view of limited government after it had been set in motion under his two terms as President.

### A. Constitutional Checks and Balances to Prevent Despotism

He explains that in a free country, the government leaders must "confine themselves within their respective Constitutional spheres",

It is important, likewise, that the habits of thinking in a free Country should inspire caution in those entrusted with its administration, to confine themselves within their respective Constitutional spheres; avoiding in the exercise of the Powers of one department to encroach upon another. The spirit of encroachment tends to consolidate the powers of all the departments in one, and thus to create whatever the form of government, a real despotism. A just estimate of that love of power, and proneness to abuse it, which predominates in the human heart is sufficient to satisfy us of the truth of this position. The necessity of reciprocal checks in the exercise of political power; by dividing and distributing it into different depositories, and constituting each the Guardian of the Public Weal against invasions by the others, has been evinced by experiments ancient and modern; some of them in our country and under our own eyes. To preserve them must be as necessary as to institute them. If in the opinion of the People, the distribution or modification of the Constitutional powers be in any particular wrong, let it be corrected by an amendment in the way which the Constitution designates. But let there be no change by usurpation; for though this, in one instance, may be the instrument of good, it is the customary weapon by which free governments are destroyed. The precedent must always greatly overbalance in permanent evil any partial or transient benefit which the use can at any time yield.

## B. The Inevitability and Danger of Partisan Politics

In his Farewell, Washington also addresses the partisan politics. He sees political parties as inevitable yet potentially dangerous. To capture this balance, he appeals to the benefits and dangers of fire:

There is an opinion that parties in free countries are useful checks upon the Administration of the Government and serve to keep alive the spirit of Liberty. This within certain limits is probably true, and in Governments of a Monarchical cast Patriotism may look with endulgence, if not with layout, upon the spirit of party. But in those of the popular character, in Governments purely elective, it is a spirit not to be encouraged. From their natural tendency, it is certain there will always be enough of that spirit for every salutary purpose. And there being constant danger of excess, the effort ought to be, by force of public opinion, to mitigate and assuage it. A fire not to be quenched; it demands a uniform vigilance to prevent its bursting into a flame, lest instead of warming it should consume.

## C. The Foundational Necessity of Religion and Morality for Political Prosperity

But with the checks and balances of the constitution and the need to manage the spirit of partisan politics, Washington lastly turns to the transcendent value of ethics grounded upon the higher law of God and inculcated by the religious organizations that flourish in a free society.

> Of all the dispositions and habits which lead to political prosperity, Religion and morality are indispensable supports. In vain would that man claim the tribute of Patriotism, who should labour to subvert these great Pillars of human happiness, these firmest props of the duties of Men and citizens. The mere Politician, equally with the pious man ought to respect and to cherish them. A volume could not trace all their connections with private and public felicity. Let it simply be asked where is the security for property, for reputation, for life, if the sense of religious obligation desert the oaths, which are the instruments of investigation in Courts of Justice? And let us with caution indulge the supposition, that morality can be maintained without religion. Whatever may be conceded to the influence of refined education on minds of peculiar structure, reason and experience both forbid us to expect that National morality can prevail in exclusion of religious principle.

> 'Tis substantially true, that virtue or morality is a necessary spring of popular government. The rule indeed extends with more or less force to every species of free Government. Who that is a sincere friend to it, can look with indifference upon attempts to shake the foundation of the fabric.

Interestingly, Washington was concerned too with the potential of a profligate citizenry and a wasteful government. Yet this did not seem a reality at his moment in time. The editor of Washington's Papers notes that in his draft of the Farewell Address:

> The words "Cultivate industry and frugality as auxiliaries to good morals and sources of private and public prosperity. Is there no room to regret that our propensity to expence exceeds our means for it? Is there not more luxury among us, and more diffusively, than suits the actual stage of our national progress? Whatever may be the apology for luxury in a country, mature in the arts which are its ministers, and the cause of national opulence. Can it promote the advantage of a young country, almost wholly agricultural, in the infancy of the arts, and certainly not in the maturity of wealth?" are crossed out. Washington has bracketed them in the margin, with the note "not sufficiently important."

Perhaps it would be good for us to remember Washington's concern about "industry", "frugality", "luxury" and "opulence" as we see the ever mounting national debt and a government that seems to spend without concern for the future well-being of the republic and even encourages its citizens not to be industrious by expansive provision of federal benefits. Generally speaking, "frugality" is not a virtue extolled by statist government for itself, although it may often be imposed upon its subjects through confiscatory taxes and extensive regulatory policies.

## D. Washington's "Vine and Fig Tree" of Religious Liberty

Washington confessed that he longed for his own "asylum" in his First Inaugural Address on April 30, 1789,

> I was summoned by my Country, whose voice I can never hear but with veneration and love, from a retreat which I had chosen with the fondest predilection, and, in my flattering hopes, with an immutable decision, **as the asylum of my declining years:** a retreat which was rendered every day more necessary as well as more dear to me.[53]

But Washington was not simply interested in himself, he desired America to be a place of Asylum for the persecuted of every nation

> ...making their Country not only an **Asylum for the oppressed of every Nation**, but a desirable residence for the virtuous and industrious of every Country.[54]
> ... the Western Country; ... which promises to afford a capacious **asylum for the poor and persecuted of the Earth**.[55]
> ... we trust the western World will yet verify the predictions of its friends and prove an **Asylum for the persecuted of all Nations**.[56]

Washington was committed to religious liberty, freedom from oppression and civil liberty. This is especially seen in his concern for the persecuted Jewish people of his day. Washington believed that there should be an asylum, or a "vine and fig tree" of safety for the Hebrew people. We see this repeatedly in his writings.[57] This asylum was also to include the people of Israel.

This **Asylum** for the persecuted of the earth was a fulfillment of the Old Testament millennial promise of peace under one's own **"vine and fig tree"**. Washington wanted America to fulfill Micah 4:4, his most frequently cited biblical text. This peace would be every American's experience under his "own vine and fig tree". Washington especially wished this vine and fig tree for the historically "oppressed" and "persecuted" Hebrew people.

He wrote on August 17, 1790 to the Hebrew Congregation in Newport Rhode Island:

> May the children of the Stock of Abraham, who dwell in this land, continue to merit and enjoy the good will of the other inhabitants, while everyone shall sit in safety under his own **vine and fig-tree**, and there shall be none to make him afraid.[58]

Washington desired the millennial peace that had been promised to Israel. To that end, he offered this blessing of his favorite Bible verse for their enjoyment of religious and civil liberty. This was the asylum Washington longed for the world to experience in the new American "promised land".[59] The freedom from religious oppression was a result of a limited government that did not impose the will of an absolute statist regime.

## VIII. THE BILL OF RIGHTS: A GUARANTEE AGAINST ABSOLUTE GOVERNMENT

As Washington's Farewell Address summarizes, the purpose of the Constitution was to outline the powers of government and to limit them by dividing them between various branches, enumerating them specifically and specifying that all the unnamed powers remain with people and the states. This is especially evident in the Bill of Rights, amendments nine and ten:

> Amendment IX: "The enumeration in the Constitution, of certain rights, shall not be construed to deny or disparage others retained by the people."

> Amendment X: "The powers not delegated to the United States by the Constitution, nor prohibited by it to the states, are reserved to the states respectively, or to the people."

But the First Amendment especially protects religious liberty and the right of the people to engage their government when it appears to them to be moving in a wrong direction:

> Amendment I: "Congress shall make no law respecting an establishment of religion, or prohibiting the free exercise thereof; or abridging the freedom of speech, or of the press; or the right of the people peaceably to assemble, and to petition the government for a redress of grievances."

The intent of the Bill of Rights is to prohibit a statist government in the United States. But if this is so, how have we come to the point where we can watch the headlong rush of our government to bind the consciences of its citizens and to pursue what appears to be the absolute rule of government over the citizens of our land?

## IX. A CONCLUDING CONSTITUTIONAL APPEAL

What then is the future of republican liberty in America? Is the erosion of the Constitution inevitable? Is the absolute hegemony of a statist government our inescapable lot? The answer depends with us. The Constitution still begins with three extraordinarily powerful and significant words: "WE THE PEOPLE". All that is necessary for evil to triumph is for good men to do nothing.

What can you and I do as the ultimate check on a government that's out of control? The first step is no longer to be "lazy". Get involved. The second is to be what Jesus taught in what Washington called, "The blessed religion revealed in the word of God". That is to be "salt and light" (Matthew 5:13-16) right where you are.

As he left the Constitutional convention, Benjamin Franklin was asked by a woman as to the kind of government that had been created by the Constitutional Convention. He answered, "A republic, madam, if you can keep it."

Ben Franklin insisted that WE THE PEOPLE must keep it alive. President George Washington agreed:

> The preservation of the sacred fire of liberty and the destiny of the
> republican model of government are justly considered as deeply,
> perhaps as finally, staked on the experiment entrusted to the hands
> of the American people." (*First Inaugural Address*, April 30, 1789).

George Washington warned us that we could lose our Constitution due to politicians' "lust for power", aided by the "human depravity" that is in all of us, and furthered by apathy or electoral laziness ("supineness of the people"). Sadly today, Washington and our Founders are generally ignored, diminished, discounted or marginalized. They are denigrated as just "old, dead, white men" that have little relevance for a post-modern world that has emerged out of decades of liberalizing progressivism. What George Washington worried about has come. It is not mere political hype or conservative hysteria. It is our reality.

**Here are some ways we are losing our Constitution:**

1. *We no longer teach it.* We are educating ourselves out of our inheritance. Jefferson said, "A nation has never been ignorant and free. That has never been and never will be." We teach "government", but we no longer teach "civics". Thus we have experienced what Bruce Cole has called "American Amnesia".

2. *We no longer read it.* When's the last time you as an American read the Constitution or heard it read? There are beginnings of Constitution readings across the country. Get involved with one. Start one. If you do, one surprise you may discover is that the phrase "the separation of church and state" is not in the Constitution! It has been read into it by the Supreme Court from a private letter of President Thomas Jefferson.

3. *We no longer honor it.* The Supreme Court's decisions are citing international law as superior to our own Constitution. This not only comprises our national sovereignty, but it diminishes our Constitution as the supreme law of our land.

4. *We no longer follow it.* The expansive interpretations of the Courts (as for example in Roe v. Wade) have in effect amended the Constitution by taking powers from the states, powers that are by the Constitution reserved for the states. The genius of the Constitution was to create a strong central government but prevent it from becoming autocratic and tyrannical by specifying its powers. The Framers sought to limit its powers to only what was specified in the Constitution. There is a procedure to amend the Constitution. But instead, our Courts have determined to make law which is contrary to the Constitution, rather than interpret law which is their constitutional duty.

5. *We as citizens no longer preserve, protect and defend the Constitution* as "We The People" — the first three words of the Constitution. The people's general political apathy has allowed their ultimate check and balance power to be compromised by creating the current equivalent of a one party system. In our inactivity, ignorance and complacence, we have become politically and spiritually lazy. We are no longer the guardians of our freedoms. The Constitution is being set aside, changed and disregarded with more and more

impunity as We The People slumber. The price of liberty is eternal vigilance. The vigilance of sleeping citizens means that liberty will slip through our national fingers and we will not even notice that it has happened.

6. *In our lethargy we enable Congress and the President to ignore the Constitution* without regard for the will of the people. The Congress recently passed legislation without voting on it. It was merely deemed to have been passed. Why would they do this? This creates law and lets the lawmakers remain unaccountable since no one knows who voted for the bill. Is this procedure permissible under the Constitution? Does the President really have the right to sign a bill into law that puts our national sovereignty at risk by saddling us and our future generations with an ever escalating and crushing debt service? Does his foresworn Constitutional duty to "preserve, protect and defend" the Constitution mean that he should not secure a national debt with a foreign power that puts our very national survival in that Country's economic policy? In America, it's not just said: "made in China". Instead it can now also be said: "owned by China". Does the Constitution give Congress and the President the power to bail out failed businesses? Does the Constitution give Congress and the President the power to impose health care on the nation even if Congress does not have the economic wherewithal to do so? Does Congress have the power to pass legislation so they can "read it to find out what's in it"?

It is my hope that we might reclaim the spirit and vision of the great American advocate of civil rights and civil liberties, the Rev. Dr. Martin Luther King Jr. In his epic *Letter From Birmingham Jail*, he wrote,

> One day the South will know that when these disinherited children
> of God[60] sat down at lunch counters, they were in reality standing
> up for what is best in the American dream and for the most sacred
> values in our Judaeo-Christian heritage,[61] thereby bringing our na-
> tion back to those great wells of democracy which were dug deep
> by the founding fathers[62] in their formulation of the Constitution[63]
> and the Declaration of Independence.[64]

It is time to stop watching liberty's death march to a thousand years of darkness under statist political absolutism. Today, begin your return to "our

Judaeo-Christian heritage, thereby bringing our nation back to those great wells of democracy which were dug deep by the founding fathers in their formulation of the Constitution and the Declaration of Independence"!

In 1838, a young Abraham Lincoln declared, "Shall we expect some transatlantic military giant to step the ocean and crush us at a blow? Never! All the armies of Europe, Asia, and Africa combined, with all the treasure of the earth (our own excepted) in their military chest, with a Bonaparte for a commander, could not by force take a drink from the Ohio or make a track on the Blue Ridge in a trial of a thousand years. At what point then is the approach of danger to be expected? I answer. If it ever reach us it must spring up amongst us; it cannot come from abroad. If destruction be our lot we must ourselves be its author and finisher. As a nation of freemen we must live through all time or die by suicide."

If we are to become the United "Statists" of America, truly, WE THE PEOPLE have only ourselves to blame.

-------------------------

*Dr. Peter A. Lillback is Professor of Historical Theology and President of Westminster Theological Seminary in Philadelphia as well as the President of The Providence Forum. He is an ordained Teaching Elder in the Presbyterian Church in America (PCA).*

[1] http://www.monticello.org/site/jefferson/government-big-enough-give-you-everything-you-wantquotation

[2] The word "statism" (and its adverbial form "statist") is a bit of a neologism. Its meaning can be summarized in the following way. The word "state" refers to centralized executive authority (administration of laws and maintenance on what is sometimes called "monopoly on violence" -- police and military establishments). Thus the words "statism" and "statist" describe institutions and political practices in which executive authority gathers increasing levels and varieties of power into its hands.

**Such executive power neutralizes the remarkable institutional creations of the liberal era ("parliaments" or democratic "representative bodies", civil liberties, independent courts and regional governing bodies within a federated hierarchy of institutions).**

Statist executive or managerial authority side-steps traditional "Western" notions of independent judicial authority. Even when it extols "rule of law", statism means obedience to regulations handed down by the state [the nation-state]. However prescriptive and however exempt it is itself from legal restraint, statist power has an inclination to insist on its version of "rule of law". The choice of "rule" rather than "governance" in this famous phrase is significant. From: http://pages.uoregon.edu/kimball/sttism.htm

[3] Karl Marx, Selected Writings, ed. David McLellan, Oxford University Press, 1977, pp. 221-47.

[4] Ibid., p. 222.

[5] Ibid., pp. 222ff.

[6] Ibid.

[7] Ibid.

[8] Madison, James, in *The Complete Madison: His Basic Writings*, ed. Saul K. Padover. (New York: Harper & Brothers, 1953), p. 335.

[9] *Writings of George Washington*, Vol. 30, 4-1789).

[10] http://townhall.com/columnists/calthomas/2015/02/19/chris-cuomo-our-rights-do-not-come-from-god-n1959137/page/full

[11] This entry from a French "Encyclopedie" labeled "mot Theiste" is found in early American patriot Joel Barlow's notes that well reveals the atheistic antipathy for theism:

> Questions. If man in all ages and countries had understood astronomy and physics as well as they do now generally in Europe would the ideas of God and religion have ever come into their minds?
>
> Have not these ideas been greater sources of human calamity than all other moral causes?
>
> Is it not necessary in the nature of things that they should be so, as long as they exist in the minds of men in such a strong degree as to form the basis of education?
>
> If we admit that these ideas are wholly chimerical having arisen altogether from ignorance of natural causes is it not the duty of every person who sees this evil tendency to use his influence to banish them as much as possible from society?
>
> Is it not possible wholly to destroy their influence and reduce them to the rank of other ancient fables to be found only in the history of human errors?
>
> If the existence of philosophy would have prevented their existence why shall it not destroy them?
>
> (Letter Books notebook (13) of Joel Barlow, "Notes on the History of Religion, Atheism, 'The Genealogy of the Tree of Liberty, The History of Algiers., etc."

[12] *Journals of Congress*, March 1776, pp. 208-09.

[13] *Journals of Congress*, November, 1777, pp. 854-55. For other examples of days of fasting and prayer, compare *Journals of Congress*, June 12, 1775; December 11, 1776; March 1778; March 20, 1779; March 1780; March 1781; March 1782. The last paragraph of the Proclamation in March 1782 is most remarkable because of the interest of the Congress in the expansion of the religion of Jesus Christ. It says, ". . .that He would incline the hearts of all men to peace, and fill them with universal charity and benevolence, and that the religion of our Divine Redeemer, with all its benign influences, may cover the earth as the waters cover the seas." (*Journals of Congress*, March 1782, p. 138.) The Thanksgiving proclamations can be found *idem.*, November 1778; October 1779; October 18, 1780; October 26, 1781; October 1782; October 18, 1783; August 1784. From these several Thanksgiving Proclamations, note the clear emphasis upon Christianity: (1779), ". . .and above all, that he hath diffused the glorious light of the gospel, whereby, through the merits of our gracious Redeemer, we may become the heirs of his eternal glory. . . .prayer for the continuance of his favor and protection to these United States; to beseech him. . .that he would grant to his church the plentiful effusions of divine grace, and pour out his holy spirit on all ministers of the gospel; that he would bless and prosper the means of education, and spread the light of Christian knowledge through the remotest corners of the earth. . . ." (1780), ". . .to cherish all schools and seminaries of education, and to cause the knowledge of Christianity to spread over all the earth." (1782), ". . . to testify their gratitude to God for his goodness, by a cheerful

obedience to his laws, and by promoting, each in his station, and by his influence, the practice of true and undefiled religion, which is the great foundation of public prosperity and national happiness." (This was written by John Witherspoon, a Presbyterian Minister from New Jersey, a member of Congress and the only clergyman to sign the Declaration of Independence.) (1783), ". . .and above all, that he hath been pleased to continue to us the light of the blessed gospel, and secured to us in the fullest extent the rights of conscience in faith and worship. . . .to smile upon our seminaries and means of education, to cause pure religion and virtue to flourish. . . ." (1784), "And above all, that he hath been pleased to continue to us the light of gospel truths, and secured to us, in the fullest manner, the rights of conscience in faith and worship."

[14] John T. McNeill, "Calvinism and European Politics in Historical Perspective in *Calvinism and the Political Order*, ed. George L. Hunt (Philadelphia: The Westminster Press, 1965), pp. 36-37. McNeill, John T. "The Democratic Element in Calvin's Thought." *Church History* 18, no. 3 (1949): 153–71.

[15] John T. McNeill, "Calvinism and European Politics in Historical Perspective in *Calvinism and the Political Order*, ed. George L. Hunt (Philadelphia: The Westminster Press, 1965), pp. 23-24.

[16] Paul T. Fuhrmann, "Philip Mornay and the Huguenot Challenge to Absolutism" in *Calvinism and the Political Order*, ed. George L. Hunt (Philadelphia: The Westminster Press, 1965), p. 50.

[17] Yardeni, "French Calvinist Political Thought, 1534–1715," 320–24.

[18] This section reflects a portion of a forthcoming article entitled, "The Relationship of Church and State" in a volume on the Protestant Reformation edited by Matthew Barrett to be published by Crossway.

[19] "Resistance Theory" by Robert M. Kingdon in *The Oxford Encyclopedia of the Reformation*, ed. Hans J. Hillerbrand, (Oxford, 1996), Vol. 3, pp. 423-425.

[20] Fuhrmann, "Philip Mornay and the Huguenot Challenge to Absolutism," 48–49.

[21] "Resistance Theory" by Robert M. Kingdon in *The Oxford Encyclopedia of the Reformation*, ed. Hans J. Hillerbrand, (Oxford, 1996), Vol. 3, pp. 423-425.

[22] Yardeni, "French Calvinist Political Thought, 1534–1715," 320–24.

[23] McNeill, "Calvinism and European Politics in Historical Perspective," 16–17.

[24] "Resistance Theory" by Robert M. Kingdon in *The Oxford Encyclopedia of the Reformation*, ed. Hans J. Hillerbrand, (Oxford, 1996), Vol. 3, pp. 423-425; Fuhrmann, "Philip Mornay and the Huguenot Challenge to Absolutism," 47–49.

[25] Skinner, *The Foundations of Modern Political Thought*, 2:334.

[26] Ibid.

[27] The St. Bartholmew's Day Massacre is a key event in French history which influenced Huguenots' political views. At the eve of St. Barthomelomew's day, on August 24, 1972, the Huguenot leader, Gaspard de Coligny was murdered in Paris and thousands other Huguenots were killed alongside him in France. Yardeni asserts, "What characterized French Calvinist political thought between the Conspiracy of Amboise and the massacre of St Bartholomew was a slide from the *right* to resist to the *duty* to resist ..." Yardeni, "French Calvinist Political Thought, 1534–1715," 319.

[28] Ibid., 321.

[29] Fuhrmann, "Philip Mornay and the Huguenot Challenge to Absolutism," 64.

[30] J. H. Burns, "John Knox and Revolution, 1558," *History Today* 8 (1958): 565ff.; Richard G. Kyle, *Theology and Revolution in the Scottish Reformation* (Grand Rapids, MI: Baker, 1980). John R. Gray, "The Political Theory of John Knox," Church History 8, no. 2 (1939): 132–47; Richard L. Greaves, "John Knox and the Covenant Tradition," *Journal of Ecclesiastical History* 24 (January 1973): 23–32.

[31] S. A. Burrell, "The Covenant Idea as a Revolutionary Symbol: Scotland, 1596–1637," *Church History* 27, no. 4 (December 1958): 338–50.

[32] J. F. Maclear, "Samuel Rutherford: The Law and the King," in *Calvinism and the Political Order*, ed. George L. Hunt (Philadelphia: Westminster Press, 1965), 72–73.

[33] Allen, *A History of Political Thought in the Sixteenth Century*, 210–30 (Puritans); Patrick Collinson, *The Elizabethan Puritan Movement* (Berkeley: University of California Press, 1967); Wiliam Haller, *Liberty and Reformation in the Puritan Revolution* (New York: Columbia University Press, 1955); Perry Miller, and Thomas H. Johnson, eds., *The Puritans* (New York: American Book Company, 1938); Richard Schlatter, ed., *Richard Baxter and Puritan Politics* (New Brunswick, NJ: Rutgers University Press, 1957); A. Craig Troxel, and Peter J. Wallace, "Men in Combat over the Civil Law: 'General Equity' in WCF 19.4," *Westminster Theological Journal* 64, no. 2 (Fall 2002): 307–18; L. John Van Til, *Liberty of Conscience: The History of a Puritan Idea* (Nutley, NJ: Craig, 1972).

[34] Allen, *English Political Thought*, 1603–1660; Robley J. Johnston, "A Study in the Westminster Doctrine of the Relation of the Civil Magistrate to the Church," *Westminster Theological Journal* 12, no. 1 (November 1949): 13–29; idem, "A Study in the Westminster Doctrine of the Relation of the Civil Magistrate to the Church (Continued)." *Westminster Theological Journal* 12, no. 2 (May 1950): 121–35.

[35] John William Allen, *English Political Thought*, 1603–1660 (London: Methuen & Co., 1938); idem, *A History of Political Thought in the Sixteenth Century*, 121ff. (England), 210–30; J. Wayne Baker, "John Owen, John Locke, and Calvin's Heirs in England," in Peter De Klerk, ed., *Calvin and the State* (Grand Rapids, MI: Calvin Studies Society, 1993), 83–102.

[36] Zacharias Ursinus, *The Commentary of Dr. Zacharias Ursinus on the Heidelberg Catechism*, trans. G. W. Williard (1852; repr., Phillipsburg, NJ: Presbyterian and Reformed, n.d.), 285–303 and 440–63; Charles D. Gunnoe, *Thomas Erastus and the Palatinate: A Rennaissance Physician in the Second Reformation*, Brill's Series in Church History 48 (Leiden: Brill, 2011); Ruth Wesel-Roth, *Thomas Erastus. Ein Beitrag zur Geschichte der reformierte Kirche und zur Lehre von der Staatssouveränität* (Lahr: M. Schauenburg, 1954); Bard Thompson, "Historical Background of the Catechism," in *Essays on the Heidelberg Catechism* (Philadelphia: United Church, 1963).

[37] Thomas Rees, ed., *The Racovian Catechism, with Notes and Illustrations* (London: Longman, Hurst, Rees, Orme, and Brown, Paternoster Row, 1818); Dariusz M. Bryćko, *The Irenic Calvinism of Daniel Kalaj (d. 1681): A Study in the History and Theology of the Polish-Lithuanian Reformation*, Refo500 Academic Studies (Göttingen: Vandenhoeck & Ruprecht, 2012).

[38] P. S. Gerbrandy, *National and International Stability: Althusius, Grotius, van Vollenhoven* (London: Oxford University Press, 1944); W. Robert Godfrey, "Church and State in Dutch Calvinism," in *Through Christ's Word*, ed. by W. R. Godfrey and J. L. Boyd III (Phillipsburg, NJ: Presbyterian and Reformed, 1985), 223–43; Nicolaas H. Gootjes, *The Belgic Confession: Its History and Sources*, Texts and Studies in Reformation and Post-Reformation Thought (Grand Rapids, MI: Baker, 2007); Daniel J. Elazar and John Kincaid, eds., *The Covenant Connection: From Federal Theology to Modern Federalism* (Lanham, MD: Lexington Books, 2000), 71–99; John Christian Laursen and Cary J. Nederman, eds., *Beyond the Persecuting Society: Religious Toleration before the Enlightenment* (Philadelphia: University of Pennsylvania Press, 1988); James W. Skillen, "From Covenant of Grace to Tolerant Public Pluralism: The Dutch Calvinist Contribution".

[39] John T. McNeill, "Calvinism and European Politics in Historical Perspective," in *Calvinism and the Political Order*, ed. George L. Hunt (Philadelphia: Westminster Press, 1965), 17.

[40] Samuel Rutherford, *A Free Disputation Against Pretended Liberty of Conscience* (London: Printed by R. I. for Andrew Crook, 1649); idem, *Lex, Rex, or the Law and the Prince* (1644; repr., Harrisonburg, VA: Sprinkle Publications, 1982); Crawford Gribben, "Samuel Rutherford and Liberty of Conscience," *Westminster Theological Journal* 71, no. 2 (Fall 2009): 355–73; John L. Marshall, "Natural Law and the Covenant: The Place of Natural Law in the Covenantal Framework of Samuel Rutherford's Lex, Rex" (Ph.D. diss., Westminster Theological Seminary, Philadelphia, 1995); Andries Raath and Shaun de Freitas, "Theologically United and Divided: The Political Covenantalism of Samuel Rutherford and John Milton," *Westminster Theological Journal* 67, no. 2 (Fall 2005): 301–21; John Coffey, *Politics, Religion*

*and the British Revolutions: The Mind of Samuel Rutherford*, Cambridge Studies in Early Modern British History (New York: Cambridge University Press, 1997); Christopher Hill, *Intellectual Origins of the English Revolution* (Oxford: Clarendon Press, 1965).

[41]  Maclear, "Samuel Rutherford: The Law and the King," 77–78.

[42]  J. F. Maclear, "Samuel Rutherford: The Law and the King," in *Calvinism and the Political Order*, ed. George L. Hunt (Philadelphia:  The Westminster Press, 1965), 75.

[43]  Samuel Rutherford, *Lex rex: the Law and the Prince. A Dispute for the Just Prerogative of King and People.  Containing the Reasons and Causes of the Most Necessary Defensive Wars of the Kingdom of Scotland, and of their Expedition for the Ayd and Help of their Dear Brethren of England* (London, 1644), 101–2.

[44]  Johannes Althusius, *Politica Methodice Digesta of Johannes Althusius*, ed. Carl J. Friedrich, Reprint of the Third Enlarged and Revised Edition of 1614 (Cambridge, MA: Harvard University Press, 1932); Carl J. Friedrich, *Johannes Althusius und sein Werk im Rahmen der Entwicklung der Theorie von der Politik* (Berlin: Duncker und Humblot, 1975; Otto von Gierke, *The Development of Political Theory*, trans. Bernard Freyd (New York: Fertig, 1966); Thomas O. Hueglin, *Early Modern Concepts for a Late Modern World: Althusius on Community and Federalism* (Waterloo, ON: Wilfred Laurier University Press, 1999; idem, "Covenant and Federalism in the Politics of Althusius; James Skillen, "The Political Theory of Johannes Althusius," *Philosophia Reformata* 39 (1974): 170–90.

[45]  McNeill, "Calvinism and European Politics in Historical Perspective," 17–18.

[46]  Hueglin, "Covenant and Federalism in the Politics of Althusius," 34.

[47]  Hueglin, "Covenant and Federalism in the Politics of Althusius," 34–35.

[48]  McNeill, "Calvinism and European Politics in Historical Perspective," 34.

[49]  Althusius, *Politics*, 134.

[50]  Hugo Grotius, *De Iure Belli ac Pacis libri tres* (1625), ed. Richard Tuck, From the edition by Jean Barbeyrac, 3vols. (Indianapolis, IN: Liberty Fund, 2005); E. Dumbauld, *The Life and Legal Writings of Hugo Grotius* (Norman, OK, 1969); W. S. M. Knight, *The Life and Works of Hugo Grotius* (London, 1925; repr., New York and London, 1962).

[51]  McNeill, "Calvinism and European Politics in Historical Perspective," 18.

[52]  Ashcraft, Richard (1986), *Revolutionary Politics and Locke's "Two Treatises of Government"*, Princeton: Princeton University Press; Huyler, Jerome (1995), *Locke in America: The Moral Philosophy of the Founding Era*, Lawrence: University Press Of Kansas, Laslett, Peter (1956); "The English Revolution and Locke's 'Two Treatises of Government'"; *Cambridge Historical Journal* 12 (1): 40–55. Waldron, Jeremy (2002), *God, Locke, and Equality: Christian Foundations in Locke's Political Thought*, Cambridge: Cambridge University Press; Zuckert, Michael. P. (2002), *Launching Liberalism: On Lockean Political Philosophy*, Lawrence: University Press of Kansas.

[53]  First Inaugural Address on April 30, 1789.

[54]  To THE MECHANICAL SOCIETY OF BALTIMORE, Philadelphia, June, 1793.

[55]  To THOMAS JEFFERSON Mount Vernon, August 31, 1788.

[56]  To JOSEPH MANDRILLON Mount Vernon, August 29, 1788.

[57]  Other examples of "asylum" are the following: To REVEREND FRANCIS ADRIAN VANDER-KEMP, Mount Vernon, May 28, 1788, To MARQUIS DE CHASTELLUX Mount Vernon, April 25[-May 1], 1788, TO THOMAS JEFFERSON Mount Vernon, January 1, 1788, To LUCRETIA WILHEMINA VAN WINTER  Mount Vernon, March 30, 1785, FAREWELL ORDERS TO THE ARMIES OF THE UNITED STATES Rock Hill, near Princeton, November 2, 1783, GENERAL ORDERS Friday, April 18, 1783.

[58]  There are some thirty examples of Washington's appeal to the "vine and fig tree" in his letters.

[59]  To MARQUIS DE LAFAYETTE, Mount Vernon, July 25, 1785

[60] The theological tension in the phrase "disinherited children of God" is palpable. The blacks had been disinherited by the whites of the South through the policy of segregation. Nevertheless, they were still children of God, and thus were entitled to the divine inheritance. God's adoption was holding fast, even while man's rejection and disinheriting was the stated policy. This is an echo of John 1:11-12, "He came unto his own, an dhis own received him not. But as many as received him, to them gave he power to become the sons of God, even to them that believe on his name." (KJV).

[61] Dr. King's "...the most sacred values in our Judaeo-Christian heritage" is an ironic statement since both Christian and Jewish clergymen were the immediate recipients of his *Letter*. The core idea of the Judaeo-Christian heritage is the belief that the one true God has given His people the true revelation of Himself seen especially in the Ten Commandments that define true worship and true justice. The phrase itself does not argue that Judaism and Christianity are the same. Rather, it implies that the core values and beliefs of America emerge from the teachings of the Old Testament prophets and the New Testament teachings of Jesus Christ. These values have created the culture of America that has enabled the great success of American liberty and law which are expressed in the political structures created by the Declaration of Independence and US Constitution. The phrase "Judaeo-Christian" also has been employed to broaden American culture's description of its history. While America began as a largely Protestant and Christian nation, over time it has welcomed the contributions of the Jewish immigrants, and thus the phrase seeks to avoid an implicit or unintended anti-Semitism. Finally, the term has become even more relevant for many as American culture has engaged the twin forces of secularism and atheism and also encountered the hostilities of Islamic *Jihad* as manifested in the September 11 terrorist attacks upon the US.

[62] Dr. King's phrase, "...great wells of democracy which were dug deep by the founding fathers" shows his belief that ultimately justice would emerge from the democratic system that the founders initiated. For example, the Declaration of Independence's assertion in 1776 that, "we are endowed by our creator with certain unalienable rights" certainly has direct application to African Americans. But the truth of this deeply dug well of democracy did not become a reality for African Americans for two more centuries. Thus Dr. King's seeming radicalism in challenging segregation in his mind was grounded in his understanding of the democratic foundations of America.

[63] Dr. King's phrase, "...their formulation of the Constitution" is simultaneously ironic and accurate. The irony is that the US Constitution began as a compromise between free and slave states. Thus the slave was not given the full dignity of personhood by the Constitution out of deference to both the northern and southern states. For the North, the compromise was reached that a slave was valued at only three fifths of a person that kept the south from having too many people for voting purposes so the southern and northern states were more equally represented in congress. For the south, the compromise was in the simple fact that slavery was allowed to continue. The framers of the Constitution believed that there would have been no Constitution if the compromise over slavery had not been accepted. It took the horrific bloodshed of the Civil War to resolve the issue. Nevertheless, Dr. King's Americanism is clear in that his hope was that the process of desegregation would in effect include the African-American in the opening language of the US Constitution, "WE THE PEOPLE", not as three fifths of a person, not as slaves, not as theoretically freed citizens who had nevertheless been denied their civil rights, but as fully functioning members and citizens of the United States under its Constitutional government exercising and enjoying the full privilege of its Bill of Rights.

[64] For a full study of The Letter From Birmingham Jail, see my *Annotations on a Letter that Changed the World from a Birmingham Jail* published by The Providence Forum in 2013.

# STATISM IN THE CHURCH

## BY CHARLIE RODRIGUEZ

IS IT POSSIBLE THAT STATIST TENDENCIES have even infiltrated the Church? Unfortunately, it is not only possible, it happens with alarming frequency.

R.C. Sproul defines statism as a:

> ". . . philosophy or worldview. A decline from statehood to statism happens when the government is perceived as or claims to be the ultimate reality. This reality then replaces God as the supreme entity upon which human existence depends."

Like the individual and the state, the Church also has a philosophy or worldview. As such, a Church governmental structure itself (whether Episcopal, Presbyterian, Congregational) is not the revealed Word of God. So it stands to reason, because the structure (form of church government) itself is man-made, and not inerrant or infallible, that it too is subject to the consequences of sin.

The sin of statism in Church governments—and even the doctrine of its spirituality—happens when that government "is perceived as or claims to be the ultimate reality," (Sproul) rather than the authority of Holy Scripture.

Beginning in the middle of the nineteenth century, with the issue of slavery as a hotly debated topic, church leaders began to take the position that the church should not involve itself in matters of the state—that it should concern itself with spiritual matters only. This position neatly allowed the church to support those in its membership who considered slaves as less than human. Today, as we look back at this misuse and misunderstanding of the "doctrine of the spirituality of the Church," two things should be clear and certain: a spirituality doctrine, which is true to Scripture, is one with no ambiguity and one which never precludes the Church (and individual clergy and members) from addressing, in or out of the Church, the biblically-based moral issues of the day (redefining marriage, abortion, stealing, lying, etc.).

Not to address such issues is never sanctioned by Scripture. Never! Not to do so also allows the state and culture to define what is moral, rather than a Holy God through Special Revelation. Thus, both the state's view apart from Scripture, and a Church doctrine which avoids "politicized moral issues"— but nonetheless biblically moral issues—these entities evolve very quickly into statist views. Why? Because "this reality then replaces God as the supreme entity upon which human existence depends." (Sproul)

Contributing factors to sinfulness within Church governments and doctrinal formulations, and the propensity and temptation to speak ex cathedra (apart from God's Word) are:

1. Power and money
2. Political correctness
3. Fearfulness
4. Lack of understanding
5. Lack of wisdom
6. Complacency

Historically, and in our present day, the Church has often retreated into a "spirituality" not found in Scripture. So, it is well worth noting Matthew Henry's teaching in his commentary on James 2:14ff with regard to faith and works:

*A justifying faith cannot be without works*—Matthew Henry

---------------------------

*Charlie Rodriguez, Publisher, Literary Agent, Bookseller, and Teaching Elder in the Presbyterian Church in America*

CPSIA information can be obtained at www.ICGtesting.com
Printed in the USA
LVOW08s0607130815

449655LV00002BA/3/P